The Image of God

The Image of God

Israel Kim

All Scripture quotations unless otherwise marked are taken from The New King James Version of the Holy Bible. Copyright © 1979, 1980, 1982, Thomas Nelson, Inc., Publishers.

Printed in Korea.

Publishing services by Selah Publishing Group, LLC, Indiana. The views expressed or implied in this work do not necessarily reflect those of Selah Publishing Group.

ISBN: 1-58930-150-1
Library of Congress Control Number: 2005925156

ACKNOWLEDGEMENTS

First and foremost, I would like to thank my Lord and Savior Jesus Christ. He has been faithful and will always continue to be faithful. I thank Him for the revelation that He has shared with me.

To my wife, Rebekah, and my daughter, Gloria: Without your support, I would not have been able to write this book or do anything else. Thank you for your love and patience. I love both of you so dearly that words can't express my feelings. I'm so blessed to be a husband and father to two such wonderful people.

To my spiritual fathers: Thank you for speaking into my life. Your love and example have made a tremendous impact on my life. Your commitment to the Gospel has brought renewed passion into my life. Thank you for being such a great spiritual father figure to me.

To my spiritual son, Israel Jacob Kim: I appreciate all your effort and help in putting this book together. Thank you for your commitment and dedication to the work of the Kingdom. May you receive double—and more than double—of the anointing in your life.

ACKNOWLEDGEMENTS

To my spiritual family (other sons and daughters): I thank God every time that I think of you. You have been a great blessing to me, and your commitment and dedication have been a powerful encouragement to me. May your family and ministry be fruitful, and may you continue to do great exploits for the Kingdom of God.

To my friends and colleagues: I am so grateful that we can build such great relationships in the Lord. I pray that we may all continue to work together to build His Kingdom in the years to come.

CONTENTS

ENDORSEMENTS

Israel Kim is an energetic and dedicated apostolic leader who has been making an unmistakable mark on his generation for years. Now, his passion to equip believers and leaders for their destiny has produced another gift for us all: "The Image of God." Thanks, Israel, for sharing your message with the world through this insightful book.

Dr. David Cannistraci
GateWay City Church, San Jose, California, USA
President of IMPACT School of Ministry

Do you want to fulfill the destiny that God has prepared for you? Do you want to live a life of victory and prosperity? If you do, Israel Kim has given us the road map to move forward in that direction in his uplifting book, *The Image of God.* This powerful book can change your life!

C. Peter Wagner, Chancellor
Wagner Leadership Institute
President of Global Harvest Ministries, Colorado
Springs, Colorado, USA

In his book, "Image of God," Apostle Israel Kim attempts to take the reader on a bold journey, similar to the journey Moses took the children of Israel on many thousands of years ago. The author has surveyed the landscape of modern Christianity and has seen many still in bondage to old ideas of the past that hinder them from the Promised Land that God has for them today. I recommend this book to the spiritually hungry. It will stimulate you to investigate for you God's calling upon you personally, as well as upon the entire church, in these last days.

Elmer Inafuku
Rhema School of the Bible Professor
Pastor of Shinjuku Shalom church, Tokyo, Japan

The Image of God masterfully leads you on a journey to understand your purpose and true identity. It is faith filled and challenging with thought provoking questions about life that pierce your very soul and cause you to seek the answers so you can walk in joy, power, love and authority. Become infused with new strength and courage to run the race as you pursue your purpose with confidence in your anointing.

Tommi Femrite
President of Gatekeepers International, Colorado
Springs, Colorado, USA
Co-Author "Intercessors: Discover your Prayer Power

In this day, when a decline of hope has filled the hearts of many Christians, Apostle Kim's book will be instrumental in rekindling the power and presence of God in our lives. As we find our identity in Him there will be an awakening in us of those things that belong to us [our inheritance]. As we renew our mind concerning the things of God, a great confidence will arise and stir that anointing that has lain dormant within us. With great confidence I encourage you to embrace the heart of this book that Apostle Kim has written, and let the winds of change remove the old mindsets and usher in a fresh revelation of God's heart and purpose for you in this hour. As you do, the Christ within will be released in a new dimension and His Kingdom will be advanced in this generation.

Apostle C.W. Clayton
Founder & President of Apostolic Resource Ministries,
Dillsboro, Indiana, USA

The new book of apostle Israel Kim is a voice of reformation and yet filled with the love of the Father coming through the teaching of this faithful servant of God. Thank you apostle Kim, for the boldness and your commitment to bring the uncompromised message of the Kingdom to this generation.•

Apostle George P. Bakalov
Overseeing Apostle Harvest Breakthrough Network International. Eagan, Minnesota, USA
European League of Apostles (Presiding Apostle).
Sofia, Bulgaria

This book, "The Image of God", written by Apostle Israel Kim will truly bless you. Apostle Kim is a man of integrity and spiritual insight. After reading this book you will be instilled with the capabilities to fulfill the task that God has for you.

This book will not only refresh you, but will assure you of who you are in Christ. The author reveals to you that you have diplomatic immunity and kingdom authority over every situation. Remember that you can't feed your new man, old man thoughts.

May God continue to bless you a thousand times more, Apostle Kim, and everyone that reads this book. Hallelujah,

Apostle H.L. Horton
The Day Star Tabernacle International, Douglasville, Georgia, USA

This book is a mentality breaker! This is a book by a man who belongs to the new breed of apostles that God is raising up in the world today. My friend, apostle Israel Kim, combines his heavenly breakthrough insights with fresh perspectives of today from the rapidly expanding Church in Eastern Asia. Here are vital keys for having dominion in the present world. Apostle Israel writes insightfully about the restoration and releasing of the anointing to judge the world - from the position that Christ has given. I have been awed by the greatness of God during the reading of this book, this might just become a classic of the new worldwide apostolic church.

Jan-Aage Torp
Oslo Leadership Training Center Dean/ Co-President
Senior Minister of Oslo Church, Oslo, Norway

The Image of God is a must read for all meat eaters! You must have a spiritual mind and a certain level of maturity to receive what is revealed in this excellent book. Apostle Israel Kim has written a spirit-led practical and experiential book designed to help you discover and understand both God's image and your own. I encourage you to read this book and share it with others so they too can be blessed!

Apostle John P. Kelly
President, LEAD (Leadership Education for Apostolic Development) Dallas, Texas, USA

Israel Kim's book, *The Image of God*, speaks to believers who long for all the Lord has destined for them. He provokes us to break out of the *ordinary* and press into a walk with God that is *extraordinary*. Apostolic revelation will help the Body of Christ walk in her true identity. She will then be positioned to fulfill her destiny in the earth. A life of supernatural potential awaits those who embrace the truths found in this powerful book. *The Image of God* will challenge the Church to live – really live – in the likeness and image of the Lord Jesus Christ!

Barbara Wentroble
Founder / Apostle
International Breakthrough Ministries,
Dallas, Texas, USA
Author – *Prophetic Intercession, God's Purpose for Your Life, You Are Anointed, People of Destiny, Praying with Authority*
Contributing Author – *Spirit Filled Women's Devotional Bible*

It is said that a man can stand anything as long as he can stand himself. No other factor is more decisive in people's psychological and spiritual development and motivation than the value judgments they make about themselves. The nature of self-evaluation has a profound effect on a person's values, beliefs, thinking processes, feelings, needs, and goals. It is clear that a person's self-esteem is the single most significant key to a person's *behavior*.

The body of Christ has suffered in its performance for too long. Apostolic leaders around the world have discovered that their sons only succeed to the level of their view of themselves. It is interesting that the business arena has understood this far better than the children of light. Our author is not suggesting and internal change through human ingenuity; but rather, a transformation through the revelation of the word of God.

Israel Kim is an apostolic father with a great passion for Christ's church. His Book, The Image of God, reflects his deep desire for the church to see itself in the image of its creator. Only then can we fulfill our God given mission!

Apostle Kim revisits the foundational truths that are vital to the structuring and empowering the church for optimal effectiveness. He unfolds the plan of God in a simple manor that allows us to reconcile our history and embrace our destiny.

He identifies the core of our weakness and offers us a real solution.

In an era when there is no shortage of *analyzing the problem* with the church, Kim offers a simple and *refreshing antidote* to the poison that has overwhelmed much of the body of Christ. Like the serpent that was lifted up in the wilderness, we only need to *look* at what the scripture offers as a cure. Kim gives us new eyes to see who we truly are (John 2:14; Numbers 21:4-9).

Bishop Flynn Johnson
Fonder/ Senior Minister of Atlanta Metropolitan
Cathedral, Atlanta, Georgia, USA

Board of Kingdom Ministries International, Coalition of Apostles, International Evangelical Churches.
Author of the His Passion for People.
Transition the Local Church from Program Based to Cell Driven.

The Image of God by Israel Kim is designed to help you answer the question, "Do I really know who I am, and am I capable of fulfilling the task God has for me?" Too many Christians don't know their identity in Christ. The result is that they cannot act out their true identity with authority. This book will help you understand your call and position in Christ, and the anointing God wants you to walk in. Kim sums it up this way... "Knowing your identity can bring you to your ultimate destination. It is the driving force in your life that will give you the assurance of what life is really all about!" If you are seeking to discover your call, purpose, and destiny, this book is for you

Apostle Chuck D. Pierce
President, Glory of Zion International Ministries, Inc.
Denton, Texas, USA
Vice President, Global Harvest Ministries,

We live a day of challenges and spiritual cultural clashes where excellence is at battle with mediocrity, where vision and hope are being robbed by lethargy and apathy. We need a spiritual adjustment and re-alignment of kingdom order and priorities so that we can walk in the fullness of God's established authority, thus endued with His anointing to break the yokes of bondage. Israel Kim's personal journey to awaken the believer out of the status quo and into a revelation of their destiny is chronicled in his book, "The Image of God." When we understand God's purposes for proper alignment and order, then the whole body functions with greater capacity and efficiency.

Apostle Doug Stringer
Founder/ President of Turning Point Ministries International,
Somebody Cares International, Huston, Texas, USA

Solomon wrote,"…of making many books there is no end, and much study is wearisome to the flesh."(Eccl.12:12 NKJV)What distinguishes a Christian book and makes it stand out, is the character and ministry of the author. Dr. Israel Kim is a pacesetter in the rapidly expanding new understanding of present day Apostolic Ministry. When he declares that the Lord assigned him to write this book, I believe him!

Dr. Kim further tells us that this book is a gathering of revelations and insights given by the Holy Spirit over the years of his ministry. That deeply stirs me to read and study what he has written. The subject of The Image of God is a must understanding for today's believer. I highly recommend this book.

Dr. Rick C. Howard,

Apostolic and Missions Pastor, Peninsula Christian Center, Redwood City, California

Author of The Judgment Seat of Christ, The King Describes His Kingdom, and The Finding Times of God

INTRODUCTION

Have you ever wondered who you were? Many people don't know who they really are in Christ. Knowing who you are in Christ will help you to both see and live life in a different way. God has a purpose for your life. He wants to use each and every one of us to shake this world upside down for the Lord. But before you can begin to make this kind of impact, you need to find out what task God has given you to fulfill.

The question you should ask yourself is, "Do I really know who I am, and am I capable of fulfilling the task God has for me?" God has given you many promises in His Word, and you need to believe in those promises. Unfortunately, many people pray to God about certain things, but they don't really believe that God will answer. They don't believe that He will answer because they don't really know what it means to be "in Christ." The Lord had a purpose in mind when He assigned me to write this book. Too many Christians don't know their identity in Christ. If they did, they would be living in the full anointing of God.

God is ready to release His power upon our lives, and we need to be ready to receive it. We must get rid of the mindset that because we are living in this world, we can only think about what goes on in this world. Even though we are in this world physically, our minds can be focused on spiritual things—we can remain in the place where Christ is seated. In reality, this world is not our home; we are in a spiritual dimension, in which we need to see, think, live, and feel in the Spirit. This attitude should change our lifestyles. God is calling us to change our lifestyles from that of the world to that of living in the Spirit. God's command is to walk and live *by the Spirit of God*. But because many of us have failed to do that, our minds are fixated on the world.

This is the mentality that God wants to break in your life. This book will reveal to you who you are in Christ, as well as the benefits of being in Christ. It will also reveal the promises that God has made—and how they apply to you now. Throughout this book, you will learn the key to living a fruitful life. This "key" is not a profound secret that no one knows, but it is a simple truth that will help you begin to see things more clearly. As you read, my prayer is that the Holy Spirit, the anointing of God, will open your eyes and heart and help you begin to live the life that God has for you. He will lead you to the truth, and the truth will set you free. Hallelujah!

CHAPTER ONE

The Voice of God

The Revelation

It was the year 1999, and I was in the midst of preparing for the new millennium. I had set aside the months of October and November to fast, pray, and diligently seek the Lord concerning His will for the coming millennium. During these two months, the Lord spoke to me and said something profound that ultimately caused me to write this book. One quick note. The reason why this book is five years late is because of my busy travel schedules and the fact that I don't have the talent of writing books. Also, in the year 2004, at an ACEA(Apostolic Council for Educational Accountability) meeting, Apostle C. Peter Wagner asked for those who wanted to write books to come up forward to receive the impartation of writing books. I went up to the front and he laid hands on me so that I could receive the impartation. Now, I have gathered all my revelations and insights and now I am writing this book.

The Lord spoke clearly and said to me, *My people don't know how to judge the world.* I pondered this insight for some time and finally asked the Lord what He meant. He restated His reply: *My people don't know how to judge the world.* After meditating on this profound statement, I finally began to understand what He was trying to say. He wanted His people to know their identity in Him, and in knowing that, they would then know how to live. The issue of *identity* is so huge that the Lord wants people to be certain of who they are and what they are called to do. When people don't know their true identity, they can't live out what they've been created to do, that is, have "dominion over the earth."

> *God created man in His own image; in the image of God He created him; male and female He created them. Then God blessed them, and God said to them, "Be fruitful and multiply; fill the earth and **subdue it; have dominion** over the fish of the sea, over the birds of the air, and over every living thing that moves on the earth."*
> Gen. 1:27–28, emphasis mine

God gave us the power to have dominion in this world— dominion over all creation. Man was created to be in charge of everything. Do you believe that you have the power to have dominion? If you do, are you living as if you have dominion over everything in this world?

Judge What?

When God said that Christians need to judge the world, He did not mean with their mouths only. This is important because many people say things, but they do not live out what they say. They are quick to speak, but slow to act. What God wants is for His people to judge the world by their "attitudes and behavior." Their faith should be evidenced by the way they live. Christians need to live by the Word of God, which sanctifies their lives. It is not enough for us to say, "Thus saith the Lord"—we need to act upon what God says.

Be doers of the word, and not hearers only, deceiving yourselves.
James 1:22

The Bible encourages us to act out our faith. Other people need to see our attitude toward Almighty God. They need to see the reverence and holiness we give to Him. For this reason, our identity comes by the way we live. Christians must understand that they are the light of this world, and that if they want that light to shine, they must let it shine through their attitudes and behavior. The world is looking for authentic Christians. They long to experience someone with a genuine faith. We need to provide authentic role models that show the character and personality of God. Because we are the light of this world, we should be bringing people out of darkness. God does not want us to hide the light that we have: We need to let it shine brightly wherever we go.

Jesus said, "You are the light of the world. A city that is set on a hill cannot be hidden. Nor do they light a lamp and put it under a basket, but on a lampstand, and it gives light to all who are in the house. Let your light so shine before men, that they may see your good works and glorify your Father in heaven."
Matt. 5:14–16

As we let our light shine in the world, we will begin to expose the darkness. God wants you to expose the darkness wherever you go. Exposing the darkness means entering Satan's territory and demolishing everything that is in it, while saving the lives of the people. We need to expose the lies and the deception of the enemy.

Have no fellowship with the unfruitful works of darkness, but rather expose them.
Eph. 5:11

Ephesians 5:11 tells us to expose—and not participate in—the "unfruitful works of darkness." So far, Christians have been very unconvincing when it comes to exposing the darkness of this world. It is time to take a stand against all unrighteousness, not only in the church but outside of the church, as well. The world constantly seeks to fill people's minds with ungodly philosophies. The world is waiting for God's true people to shine forth and manifest His glory. People need to see His glory in our lives. But for that to happen, we ourselves need to be in the presence of the Lord daily. We must ask the Lord to restore our hunger for His Kingdom. In order for that to happen, we need to continually enter into the presence of the Lord. Without being in the presence of God daily, we will not be able to satisfy the hunger that people have. They are hungry for something real. They don't want anything that is superficial.

> *For the earnest expectation of the **creation eagerly waits***
> *for the **revealing of the sons of God.***
> ROM. 8:19, EMPHASIS MINE

The world is waiting for the revealing of the sons of God. The sons of God will be revealed. This means that people will be able to see God's children, because they will be representing the nature of God in this world. The world is waiting for this, because until that time comes, true restoration will not take place. The true sons of God will bring restoration between the world and the Creator. How will the true sons of God be manifested? They will be led by the Spirit. What will happen once the true sons of God are revealed? Heaven will be on earth, and the glory of God will cover the earth. All creation will be restored, and there will be no more disasters, but true peace on earth. What I mean by "true peace" is that nothing in creation will suffer anymore. When the true sons of God are revealed, they will have the authority to prevent all natural disasters from happening. Is this possible? Yes! Why do I say "yes"? I say "yes" because I see it in the lives of the people whom I read about in the Scriptures. If God gave them authority to speak to nature, then He definitely gave us that same authority, too, especially since we are now "in Christ." Let's take a look at three examples from God's Word.

First, God used Moses to open up the Red Sea. As Moses lifted his arms with the staff, the Red Sea was divided, and the Israelites walked forward on dry land to the other side of the sea (Exod. 14:21–22). God granted Moses authority over nature to bring about salvation for His people.

Next, we read that Joshua asked God to cause the sun to stand still and the moon to stop, and He did. Joshua used his authority to cause nature to cease at the voice of his command. The Bible says that God heeded the voice of a man (Josh. 10:12–14, esp. v. 14). This happened when God delivered the hands of the Amorites to Joshua and the Israelites.

Finally, we need to take a look at the ultimate example of our faith, Jesus. When Jesus and His disciples were in a boat, a storm rose up that caused the disciples to fear for their lives. Jesus, at this time, was fast asleep below the deck, while the disciples were above, trying to survive the storm. Because there was nothing they could do, and because the storm was getting worse, one of the disciples went down to wake Jesus up and tell Him the problem. Jesus came up to the deck, commented on the disciples' lack of faith, and then ordered the storm to be still. When He gave that order, the storm died down, and there was peace (Matt. 8:23–27; Mark 4:35–41). The disciples were shocked and wondered who Jesus really was. The true sons of God will make believers out of people because they will have authority from on high.

> For as many as are **led by the Spirit of God, these are sons of God.**
> ROM. 8:14, EMPHASIS MINE

This verse tells us that the sons of God must live by the Spirit of God. All of their actions, thoughts, motives, and behavior must be the direct result of the Spirit's leading. They need to follow what the Spirit is leading them to do. This is where we must die daily and crucify our fleshly desires. This is where we must start focusing on building the Kingdom of God rather than our own earthly kingdoms. When this happens, the sons of God will bring light to the dark areas of the world. The sons of God will become evident by their attitudes and behavior, because they will demonstrate the reality and existence of God. When God called us to judge the world, what He really meant was that we are called "to deliver the people out from the darkness." God made us deliverers. We have a task to fulfill. I will expand on this more in detail later.

Present Address in Christ

We have something inside of us that enables us to judge the world—our position in Christ. Once we know our status in Christ, we can act out our true identity with authority. The problem is that we are not seated properly. We are seated outside of His Kingdom. Because we are not preoccupied with fulfilling God's Kingdom, we are not seated with Christ in heavenly places. The Bible clearly states that we are already seated with Him in heaven:

> God, who is rich in mercy, because of His great love with which He loved us, even when we were dead in trespasses, **made us alive together with Christ** (by grace you have been saved), and **raised us up together**, and **made us sit together** in the heavenly places in Christ Jesus.
> EPH. 2:4–6, EMPHASIS MINE

Even though we may presently be here in this world, we know that our present address is sitting with Christ in heavenly places. If we are seated in heavenly places with Christ, we are meant to rule and reign over the world. God wants us to live out this reality. That is the purpose of sitting with Him: to take dominion over the world. We need to exercise this in our life.

The problem is, we all have been trained to listen to our parents or to follow the ways of this world. God wants to train us to listen to what He says. Now is the time when Christians need to hear directly from God. Many Christians say that they can't hear the voice of God. The reason may be that every time we hear men's voices, it prevents us from hearing and recognizing God's voice. We are accustomed to hear voices of people, and that confuses us when we try to hear from God because we tend to think rationally. But when we are thinking rationally, God may be speaking irrationally to us.

> *"For My thoughts are not your thoughts,*
> *Nor are your ways My ways," says the* LORD.
> *"For as the heavens are higher than the earth,*
> *So are My ways higher than your ways,*
> *And My thoughts than your thoughts."*
> ISA. 55:8–9

We try to rationalize God's words and ways and bring them down into our human thinking. That is how the world teaches us: to think rationally. To think irrationally does not work well in the human intellect. But God created us so that we can specifically know and recognize His voice. Most of us need more training in this area. Our spiritual ears need to spend more time learning to filter out rational thinking when it comes to hearing the voice of God.

> *Jesus said, "My sheep hear My voice, and I know them,*
> *and they follow me."*
> JOHN 10:27

Understand this truth: When God created us, He created us to hear Him first. When Adam and Eve were created, they had fellowship with God. That would mean that they heard the voice of God because they had an intimate relationship with Him. Do you have an intimate relationship with the Lord? If you do, then you are able to hear His voice. It was not until they heard the "rational" temptations of the serpent that they started to rationalize everything.

When we begin to listen for and only hear His voice, we will be able to follow Him because His voice will be familiar to us. Instead of becoming familiar with the voices of the world, we need to become familiar with His voice. But this will only happen when we renew our prayer life. Prayer is the key to hearing the voice of God. We need to have a hunger and a dedication to pray and wait upon the Lord. Many people just pray and then leave without hearing what God has to say. Waiting upon the Lord is an important part of prayer. Prayer should include not only what we say, but also what He says back to us. Basically, this means that when we leave God's presence early, our prayer life is shortened. But as we remain in His presence, we will also come to know His will, because we are seated and reigning with Him. That is the privilege we have in God. God designed it this way, but again, the problem is that we are not sitting with Him. There are several hindrances that prevent us from believing this truth.

1) Feelings of unworthiness

Many of us feel that we are unworthy to sit with Christ because of our flaws and sins. We try to gain merits in order to be counted worthy to sit beside Christ. We believe that we have to reach a certain level of spiritual maturity to be able to sit with Him. We tend to belittle ourselves because of our flawlessness or weaknesses. But what we need to understand is that we are already considered worthy to receive what God wants to give us.

No matter what sins or flaws you may think you have, God does not judge you by those standards. He has already found us to be righteous because we have the righteousness of Christ. That was the whole purpose of the cross. When Christ died for us, He took all of our flaws and sins upon Himself. He took everything that did not represent who He was and restored it back to us. This is what we mean by the grace of God. We can sit with Christ because of the grace of God, which enables us to be with Him.

> **There is therefore now no condemnation to those who are in Christ Jesus**, who do not walk according to the flesh, but according to the Spirit. For the law of the Spirit of life in Christ Jesus has made me free from the law of sin and death.
> ROM. 8:1–2, EMPHASIS MINE

Jesus paid the price so that we can be counted worthy. We need to stop condemning and belittling ourselves and start confessing our position in the Lord.

2) The belief that sitting with Christ is a future reality

Many people think that we will be seated next to the Lord when we get to heaven. They miss the point that "being seated" is both a present and a future reality. If you read the Bible carefully, the word *seated* is in the past tense. What that tells us is that we are *already* seated with the Lord. Even though we can't see it, we know it by faith. We must believe that we are seated with Christ, even now, in heavenly places. Many people think about the future, and believe that only in the future will we experience all these wonderful things. God did not only design blessings for the future, but He also planned them for the present. God has blessed us with all spiritual blessings *in the present*.

27

Blessed be the God and Father of our Lord Jesus Christ, **who has blessed us with every spiritual blessing in the heavenly places in Christ.**
EPH. 1:3, EMPHASIS MINE

This means that what is in heaven is ours, and what is on earth is also ours. Why is that? It's because we are seated with Him. God has positioned us to receive these blessings. If we are not seated with Him, we can't receive these spiritual blessings. Because we are seated with Him now, we can expect these spiritual blessings to be a daily part of our lives. That's why we need to be excited, filled with great expectations for God's Kingdom. Do you want to see blessings come upon your life? Then you need to expect them because of your position. Because you are sitting with the Lord, you can expect these things to occur in your life.

3) Over-spiritual attitudes

Some people *can* get overly spiritual at times. They tend to take the spiritual aspects of the Bible and symbolize or over-rationalize them. This causes an imbalance in God's Word and is done in the flesh. But God is Spirit, and He speaks to His people, who are spiritual beings. Jesus told Nicodemus that whatever is born of the flesh is flesh and whatever is born of the Spirit is Spirit (John 3:6). We have the Holy Spirit inside of us, and He helps us to understand the spiritual things pertaining to God.

God has revealed them to us through His Spirit. For the Spirit searches all things, yes, the deep things of God.
1 COR. 2:10

This is something I said before. We try to rationalize everything, because we have been trained to do so. It is through the Spirit that we worship our God. God wants us to live in the Spirit. We need to walk and live by the Spirit of God. If people think that *this* is "overly spiritual," then we have to also disregard spiritual warfare, which is clearly taught in the Bible. Paul tells us that we are in a war, and that our war is not against flesh and blood, but against spiritual beings:

> *For we do not wrestle against flesh and blood, but against principalities, against powers, against the rulers of the darkness of this age, against spiritual hosts of wickedness in the heavenly places.*
> EPH. 6:12

> *For though we walk in the flesh, we do not war according to the flesh. For the weapons of our warfare are not carnal but mighty in God for pulling down strongholds.*
> 2 COR. 10:3–4

Identity Comes from God

Now, let's go back to our identity issue. You may be asking: "Who am I?" "What am I called to do?" "What's my purpose in life?" These are simple questions we all ask ourselves, but for some the answers are difficult to figure out. Many people try to find their identity through the things they do, or in the area or circumstances by which they are surrounded. People often struggle with their calling and purpose in life, but they are turning it into a complex issue. We make it complex when we try to find our sense of self by comparing ourselves with the world. When we do that, it brings confusion: We start to rationalize everything instead of believing that God created us in His own image with a purpose. Our minds so easily begin to think in the pattern of the world's system. We go to school to get an education and find a job, get married, and live our lives until we grow old and die. People try so hard to find their sense of identity in the things they can acquire or in the things they have accomplished in life. Most people feel confident in what their hands have accomplished. But as Christians, we need to know that our identity comes directly from God. The Bible clearly states that we were created "in His own image."

> So God **created man in His own image**; in the image of
> God He created him; male and female He created them.
> GEN. 1:27, EMPHASIS MINE

To understand this verse, we need to go back to the beginning. "In His own image" contains all the treasures and resources of who we are. What does it mean to be created in the image of God? To be created in the image of God means that there is Someone living inside of you, Someone who gives life to you.

> For in Him we live and move and have our being.
> ACTS 17:28

Image of God

Before we go any further, let's dissect this phrase and determine what it means to be created "in His own image." First of all, we need to know who the image of God is. It is Christ.

> [The gospel is veiled to those] whose minds the god of
> this age has blinded, who do not believe, lest the light of
> the gospel of **the glory of Christ, who is the image of
> God**, should shine on them.
> 2 COR. 4:4, EMPHASIS MINE

Jesus said that He resembles the Father:

> "He who has seen Me has seen the Father."
> JOHN 14:9

Jesus was implying that the Father has been manifested through the Son. As people were looking at Jesus, they were also looking at the Father.

Because Christ is the image of God, He also lives inside of you. When people see you, they should see Jesus, because He is living inside of you. Many people forget this great truth. They forget who is living inside of them. If they only realized that the Creator of the world, the omnipotent God, is within them, they would see things differently. They would see the world through the eyes of God. The mentality of most Christians needs to change.

> *I have been crucified with Christ; it is no longer I who live, but **Christ lives in me**; and the life which I now live in the flesh I live by faith in the Son of God, who loved me and gave Himself for me.*
> GAL. 2:20, EMPHASIS MINE

We need to see the world through the eyes of God. When we do, we can truly die to this world and live according to our identity. We must allow Christ to live our lives for us. But this will only happen if we surrender our lives to Him. That means that whatever He desires for us to do, we will do, and this results in our living by the faith of Jesus. Every day we need to pray that we may die to this world, so that Christ will live in our lives.

> *God forbid that I should boast except in the cross of our Lord Jesus Christ, by whom the **world has been crucified to me, and I to the world**.*
> GAL. 6:14, EMPHASIS MINE

Looking Forward and Not Back

We need to be encouraged to fully trust in the Lord, because He provides everything that we need. Our problem is that we are so focused on our past that we can't go forward in life. We are not on the same pace with God because we are looking back at our lives and wondering what might have been. Instead of walking with God, we are walking behind Him. And as we walk behind

Him, we are looking back, which slows us down and affects the decisions we make in life. We wonder if the choices we made were good. But if we continue to wonder after we decide to follow Christ, it will only cause more pain and more opportunity for doubt to grow in our minds. Scrutinizing our past only reminds us of our inabilities and failures, and we are unable to see the potential that we have in Christ. We become unstable because we lose confidence.

After we accept the Lord, we must allow Him to lead us. He becomes our new confidence. This is what it means to surrender our lives to the Lord. We live to do His will, to do what He wants us to do. We maintain total trust and reliance upon Him to provide for us. We become more dependent on Him every day of our lives.

We also begin to think differently. We don't live according to the flesh, but rather, according to His faith. His faith needs to rise above all hindrances and negative aspects of our lives. The world confuses our minds, convincing us to seek significance outside of God. But life should be all about God and not about us. It is about what He has promised in our lives. We need to hold on to the promises of God. To understand life, we need to go to the One who gave us life. True life is found within the Life Giver. With this truth, we can stand straight and walk confidently. The world is not looking for people who slouch when they walk, but we can't stand tall without confidence. As you stand tall, placing your faith in the promises of God, you will become assured of everything. You will be able to see what lies ahead, and even beyond. But when we are not standing tall, we can't walk with confidence. We are allowing the things of the world to steal away our confidence in God.

Chapter Two

The Restoration of the Garden of Eden

The reason we need to know our identity is so that the Garden of Eden will be restored to us. How can the Garden be restored to us? What will it mean when the Garden is restored back to us? What was it that man had in the Garden at the beginning, and lost, but that God wants to restore? In order to answer these questions, we must first understand the significance of the "Garden of Eden."

The Garden of Eden

What is the significance of the phrase "Garden of Eden"? The word *garden* in the Hebrew language means "to protect." The word *Eden* in the Hebrew language means "pleasure and delight," as well as "rejoice." So, we need to "protect" our "joy" in life. When God created the Garden, there was only joy to be found there. Adam and Eve lived in pure joy. Nothing outside of joy was there. Constant communication with God also brought them joy. Can you live a life that constantly rejoices in the Lord? For many Christians, there is no joy in their lives. Something or someone has robbed them of experiencing this joy. This is what God wants to restore to His people. He wants to restore joy so that we can return to our main purpose in life. What God started in the beginning (a joyful relationship with Him and with others), He wants to restore to you. Many people have a relationship with the Lord, but not all of their relationships are filled with joy. If your relationship with the Lord is not filled with joy, it will quickly become an obligation. But relationships that are filled with joy give us the freedom to live life under the grace of God. Under the grace of God, we have an intimate relationship with Him.

Adam and Eve were created and placed in the Garden of Eden. There, they experienced a divine and intimate relationship with the Father. They communed with Him and walked with Him. God made their purpose clear to them: They were to do two things—"cultivate and keep" the Garden.

> Then the LORD God took the man and put him in the garden of Eden to **tend and keep** it.
> GEN. 2:15, EMPHASIS MINE

What did it mean when God told them to do these two things? The word *cultivate* in the Hebrew language is *abad*. The word means "to worship and serve." God created man in order to worship and serve Him. Man's primary purpose in life is to be a servant and a worshipper. As we worship and serve God, He reveals what His plans are for our lives. Our service to God is what gives us the joy to live life.

The word *keep* in the Hebrew language is *shamar*. This word means "to protect; to put a hedge around." God entrusted man to not only serve and worship Him, but to also protect the Garden. The serpent took that joy away from man because it was not fully *protected*. And once the serpent took the joy away, Adam's defenses were weakened. He allowed certain doors of deception to confuse his mind.

How many of us have lost our joy in life? We have been robbed of our joy because we did not protect the precious things in our lives. With what did the enemy deceive you that enabled him to steal your joy away from you? After Adam and Eve fell to the sin of deception, they lost the privilege and honor of life in the Garden. But God had a master plan to bring them back to that place.

Once you know your identity in Christ, you will begin to live a life that is different and far better than the one you have been living. We all want to live a life that is filled with adventure, but life is an adventure with God. This adventure takes place when we only have God as our Resource and Guide. He wants to lead us to where He is. He came to us, to the place we were before salvation. Now, our adventure is to go where He is, because where He is, there is freedom and restoration of life and joy.

True Meaning: What Really Happened in the Garden?

What was God's intention when He created man? His intention was to give him His anointing. When we were created, we were created in His image. We have already learned that the image of God is Christ. The word *Christ* in the Hebrew language means "Messiah; the Anointed One." Christ is the Anointed One of God. Because Christ is living inside us, His anointing is also inside of us. So, when God created man, He gave man all of the anointing. This anointing in man gave him the power and the authority to take dominion over the earth. This tells us that the anointing is the key to everything! (I will go into more detail about the anointing and what kind of anointing we have later.)

This dominion was evident when Adam named all of the animals in Genesis 2:19–20. Man had dominion over the animals. This is a revelation to us. The revelation is that God had given all power and authority to Adam. Adam had God's power and authority to take care of the Garden. Both Adam and Eve had the full anointing of God in their lives. Both of them had dominion over the earth—and also over the serpent.

The problem was that Adam did not know what he really had. If he had known what he had, he would not have been deceived, and instead, he would have rebuked the serpent that tried to trick him. But because he did not realize this, the serpent was able to deceive him, and when man was deceived, he lost everything. Do you know what you have in Christ?

If we don't know who we are in Christ, the enemy will come and deceive us. He will take away everything that is precious in our lives. He will strike at the very moment when our defenses are down, when we don't know who we are and what we have. He takes that and uses it to his advantage. Not only did Adam and Eve lose everything, but a curse fell upon their lives that brought judgment and condemnation. Because of this, man became ashamed and tried to hide from God.

> *Then the eyes of both of them were opened, and they knew that they were naked; and they sewed fig leaves together and made themselves coverings. And they heard the sound of the LORD God walking in the garden in the cool of the day, and Adam and his wife hid themselves from the presence of the LORD God among the trees of the garden. Then the LORD God called to Adam and said to him, "Where are you?" So he said, "I heard Your voice in the garden, and I was afraid because I was naked; and I hid myself."*
>
> GEN. 3:7–10

We Have the Power

The same thing happens to us today. If we don't know our true identity, we will not know what we have. And if we don't know what we have, we will continue to live the same old, powerless life. We will live in constant deception. The curse is passed down to us until we realize what is happening and get rid of it. This problem that Adam had, we now have in our lives—and in the church. The church needs to know who she is and what she has been called to do. She is filled with the power of God, but she doesn't realize the power that she has.

Jesus said, "You are Peter, and on this rock I will build My church, and the gates of Hades shall not prevail against it."
MATT. 16:18

Because the church has lost her power, people are looking to psychologists, fortune tellers, and palm readers for the answers to the questions of life. Why are people going to them instead of the church? It is because the church does not know her power or her mission. She has the answers to the world's problems, but she has lost her power to judge. But God still has a master plan. He revives us by putting His Spirit within us—the same Spirit that brought life to the dry bones (Ezek. 37). We need to be revitalized! The church today is dry and beaten-up by the world. She has lost her joy, her power, and her sense of direction. The church was destined for a great harvest, but she is not fulfilling her purpose because of the lack of knowledge of her identity. And since she lost her identity, she has been suffering from the attacks of the enemy.

The church is not "crazy" enough in this world. People don't want to come to church because they only see "normal" people in church. Christianity is not about ordinary people, but extraordinary people! When we are "crazy," the people will come and wonder why we are crazy. To act crazy in this way means that the joy inside of us is being shown forth to the world.

Chaplaincy at a Mental Institute

Several years ago, I was the chaplain of a mental institute back in Fairfax County. As soon as you walked in the door, you would see crazy things happening. People would look at you and begin to smile. They didn't know what they were doing, but they just smiled and laughed at you. They didn't care who they were or what others thought about them. They just felt free to express themselves.

We need to learn how to express ourselves without being ashamed of who we are. If the church has joy, then the people will know that we have the truth. That truth leads to the real source of blessing. We need to know that we have something for which the world is searching.

Satan knows that when we, the church, come to realize our identity, we will become his biggest adversary and threat—to both him and his kingdom. He knows that we possess the greatest weapon for demolishing strongholds. He knows that his time is limited and that when we, the church, learn how to use our weapons, he will be defeated. Our weapons give us the power and authority to take dominion and be rulers of this earth.

The Beauty of Creation

Man was created to worship God through His beautiful creation. God's creation was meant not only for our enjoyment but to cause us to focus on the Creator of all things. Man fell short of this response because he has neglected the purpose of creation. When Adam's guard was down, the serpent found an opening in which to strike. God wants us to protect what's been placed inside of us. Man is to worship God through His creation. God created everything to show forth His glory, and mankind is to acknowledge His glory. We must have the strength of character to protect what God has entrusted to us. His anointing inside of us is the key to our dominion in this world.

The Garden of Eden Restored

There are certain things that God wants to restore in your life. When Jesus died on the cross, everything that had been stolen or taken away from us was restored. The Garden of Eden was restored at the crucifixion of Jesus. Two other people were crucified with Jesus: a malefactor on His left and another criminal on His right. The malefactor on the left represented Satan. He was testing the Lord, tempting Him to save both Himself and the two men. He taunted Jesus, saying that if He were the Christ, He would be able to save Himself by coming down from the cross. In Matthew 4, Satan challenged and tempted Jesus, but it didn't stop there. The malefactor constantly hurled insults and challenged the Lord on the cross. But the criminal on the right represented Adam. He rebuked the other malefactor and defended Jesus, asserting that the Lord did not deserve this punishment. The criminal on the right repented and asked Jesus to remember him when he died, and Jesus stated that the man would be in Paradise with Him that very day.

> *Then he said to Jesus, "Lord, remember me when You come into Your Kingdom." And Jesus said to him, "Assuredly, I say to you, today you will be with Me in Paradise."*
> LUKE 23:42–43

The term *paradise* here referred to the Garden of Eden. But I want to focus on what the criminal said: He said to "remember me." The words *remember me* here in the Aramaic mean to "restore me." Jesus was restoring the man back to the Garden. That man represented Adam, and Jesus represented the second Adam. So, Adam was restored in Jesus.

How can we be restored to the Garden of Eden? We are restored as we continue to sit with Him in heavenly places. God created us to speak and declare the things that He promised for our lives. This is a crucial time for us to be restored to the Garden of Eden. God is in the process of restoration.

CHAPTER THREE

The Tree of Life

God created mankind for a purpose: to live life with joy in our hearts. Joy was given to protect our lives from any spirit of apathy or indifference. The Bible states that the joy inside of us strengthens us. It is the power by which we live:

> *"Do not sorrow, for the joy of the LORD is your strength."*
> NEH. 8:10

Our joy in the Lord will bring forth living water that will protect us from being sluggish in our lives. That living water is the Holy Spirit. The Holy Spirit should give us joy in life.

Let's take a closer look at Genesis 2:8–15. God planted the "tree of life...in the midst of the garden" (Gen. 2:9). Where is the tree of life located today? Many would answer that it is in the middle of the Garden. However, today the tree of life is not in the midst of the Garden. The tree of life is not to be found in a physical location. The tree of life is within us. Do you believe this? Let me explain what and where the tree of life really is.

Where Is the Tree of Life?

The book of Proverbs explains that the tree of life is not to be found in a physical location, but rather, it is something that is found within us. In Proverbs 3:18 (emphasis mine), the tree of life is referred to with a feminine pronoun:

She is a tree of life to those who take hold of her,
And happy are all who retain her.

Who is "she" in this passage? The word *she* refers to wisdom. Who is wisdom? Wisdom is Christ. Christ is the "wisdom of God":

> *Christ [is] the power of God and the **wisdom of God**.*
> 1 Cor. 1:24, emphasis mine

Jesus is our tree of life. Everyone who turns to Jesus will receive fullness of life.

> *Jesus said, "The thief does not come except to steal, and to kill, and to destroy. I have come that they may have life, and that they may have it more abundantly."*
> John 10:10

Jesus came to give us life—and not just life here on earth, but also life after we die. Let's first focus on life here on earth for a bit. Jesus came to give us abundance in life, which should be lived out while we're still here. God wants us to live in abundance. This abundant life is not only something we receive in the future, but it's also for our present lives. Why should we have that expectation? Because we are positioned properly (seated) with Him in heaven. We have to understand that, because of our position in Christ, we have all the blessings that God has promised to us.

The tree of life is also righteousness. Righteousness is an inner characteristic.

*The fruit of the **righteous** is a tree of life,*
And he who wins souls is wise.
PROV. 11:30, EMPHASIS MINE

We read also that the tree of life is a soothing tongue. It is a wholesome tongue that we need to guard.

*A **wholesome tongue** is a tree of life,*
But perverseness in it breaks the spirit.
PROV. 15:4, EMPHASIS MINE

The tree of life is also God's desire.

Hope deferred makes the heart sick,
But when the desire comes, it is a tree of life.
PROV. 13:12

Power of the Tongue

We see that there is life in the power of the tongue. We don't realize how powerful our words may be to other people.

Death and life are in the power of the tongue,
And those who love it will eat its fruit.
PROV. 18:21

We need to be careful how we use our tongues. We need to only speak words that will encourage and strengthen people, and not destroy them.

He who guards his mouth preserves his life,
But he who opens wide his lips shall have destruction.
PROV. 13:3

The tree of life gives life to those who are dead. We have the power to give life because the tree of life is within us. This means that Jesus Christ is within us. And because He is within us, He gives us abundant life

Have you ever noticed how the things you say to others do, in fact, affect them? For example, if you tell someone that she is fat, and continue to tell her that she is really fat, she will end up believing that. When she believes that, her lifestyle may be changed if she begins to try to lose weight. Her actions took place because you said something to her that affected her. The book of James tells us that the tongue is untamable. People have a hard time controlling the things that they say.

> *No man can tame the tongue. It is an unruly evil, full of deadly poison. With it we bless our God and Father, and with it we curse men, who have been made in the similitude of God.*
> JAMES 3:8–9

So, power rests in the words we say. We need to be careful how we use the power of our speech.

> *Jesus said, "For by your words you will be justified, and by your words you will be condemned."*
> MATT. 12:37

The one who knows how to control his tongue is wise. The Bible clearly states that we need to know how to give life to other people. Life comes from our tongues, and we need to use them properly, in the way that He wants us to use them. We need to speak words of encouragement and edification to other people, giving them life and bringing them more faith and confidence in the Lord.

CHAPTER FOUR

True Identity

Your identity does not depend on the circumstances in which you find yourself. When God calls people, He calls them according to His will and His purpose. It has nothing to do with our accomplishments, but it is totally based upon the grace and sovereignty of God. He does not differentiate according to social class, race, or gender. He calls those whom He wants to call.

Poverty Mentality

I want to explain this unbiblical truth that was and is still being taught, but which keeps people from answering the call of God on their lives. This unbiblical truth concerns the spirit of poverty. When God calls people, He does not just call poor people. These days, many people struggle with their calling because they believe that ministers must be poor in order to be in God's will. People seem to think that being poor is a sign that demonstrates their total commitment to the Gospel, especially for those who are called into full-time ministry. This unbiblical truth has limited the work of God by convincing people that being poor is a sign of humility and that they must give up everything in order to serve the Lord.

> *Beloved, I pray that you may prosper in all things and be in health, just as your soul prospers.*
> 3 JOHN 2

The Bible clearly states that God wants us to prosper in life so that we can do the work of the Kingdom. How can we advance the Kingdom of God if we ourselves are poor? God prospers us for a reason—so that we can build His Kingdom. He not only encourages us to prosper, but He also gives us the power to prosper.

> "And you shall remember the LORD your God, for it is **He who gives you power to get wealth**, that He may establish His covenant which He swore to your fathers, as it is this day."
> DEUT. 8:18, EMPHASIS MINE

It is God's desire to see His children prosper and do great exploits for the Kingdom of God with their wealth. The only stipulation we have been given regarding our wealth is to be good stewards of it. Later in this book, I will expand on the doctrine of prosperity and tell you why prosperity is an actual promise of God.

The Call

I remember the first time I went to church; I believe that I was in junior high school. When I entered the church, I saw the pastor wearing an outdated suit with an old, torn tie. At that time, I did not understand the Word of God, but I asked myself why the pastor had to be poor. I already understood that God was a big God and that He controlled the universe. He could give that pastor a new suit. Pastors who lived in poverty did not make sense to me, no matter how I thought about it. But I wanted to know the truth.

As I grew in the faith, God called me into fulltime ministry, but I tried to avoid His call. I had no plans or desire to go into fulltime ministry, especially after I had seen the poverty of pastors. Nobody wants to live life being poor and having nothing. But it seemed that pastors had to struggle each day just to get by. My primary objective and goal in life at that time was to get a Ph.D. in international business, buy lots of nice things, build a big house—and support missionaries.

As God continued to call me into ministry, I gave Him an ultimatum. I said, "If You don't bless me financially, then I won't do it." I struggled and wrestled with this for three long months. Finally, I gave in and accepted the call—without any conditions.

When God calls us, He always provides for us. He is a God who provides all the things that we need.

> And my God shall supply all your need according to His riches in glory by Christ Jesus.
> PHIL. 4:19

To receive what we need, we must look in the right place: God made us sit with Him, and our thoughts and attention should be focused on Him. Once we are focused on Him, we will never lose track of our purpose.

> If then you were raised with Christ, **seek those things which are above**, where Christ is, sitting at the right hand of God. **Set your mind on things above**, not on things on the earth. For you died, and your life is hidden with Christ in God.
> COL. 3:1–3, EMPHASIS MINE

The Vision

I remember a vision the Lord gave me a few years ago. I had already received two prophecies concerning an airplane. In the vision, God showed me and then gave me an airplane. The airplane was filled with many people whom I would take to travel around with me. The airplane was given to me in order for me to focus on team ministry. Also, in the vision, I saw massive evangelistic services. I saw myself going to many different big stadiums, preaching and seeing many miracles taking place. The stadiums were filled with many unbelievers from all different nationalities. Every stadium that I went to was filled with these different groups of people. I even saw everyone appear as black at first, but while I was preaching, their appearance started to change to white. I knew and believed that this vision would become a reality.

Wilderness Training

From that moment on, the Lord began to train me in the wilderness. He wanted me to go through the wilderness to teach me that I needed to be dependent upon Him for all of my needs in life. We all need to learn how to be dependent on God. Wilderness training teaches us to depend on God to provide the things we need in life. Time spent in the wilderness is not something we should fear or avoid, but it is a time when we experience the power of God. It is a time when God supplies all of our provisions. We need to get this idea out of our minds that the wilderness is something "empty," that it is a place where we don't receive anything. The wilderness experience is actually just the opposite. I am currently writing a book entitled *The Purpose of the Wilderness*. In that book, I explain the real truth of the wilderness.

A Need Met

I remember a time when I had no resources in my life. I was an only child, and my parents had chosen not to support me during my seminary years. At that time, I began to see God supplying my needs little by little. There was one specific instance that gave me a clear assurance of this. One day, when I went to the post office, I received an envelope full of cash with a letter that stated that the person had felt the Lord directing him to send a certain amount of money to this address. I had never met this person before! Through this situation, God showed me that He is *Jehovah Jireh*, my Provider. The Lord showed me that He will indeed provide for all of my needs. So, I continue to pray for and believe Him for an airplane of my own. The reason God is blessing me financially is so that I can build His Kingdom. If ministers are poor, how can they contribute to the Kingdom of God? When God provides for a need, He always blesses us more than we ever expected. And He wants us to bless others just as He blesses us.

The New Work of God

God is doing something special as He restores our identity in Christ. He wants the church to come to understand her true identity. Through the years, the church has taught a "corporation structure," based upon hierarchy. The church functioned as a corporation by focusing only on one person. The pastor did everything, and there was no emphasis on team ministry. Instead of forming teams, churches have been building committees, which made up the laws and rules of the church. The committees were the ones who led the church. They were the ones who elected and hired pastors, deacons, and elders. (I'm not referring to the biblical office of "elders," but to those who have been in church the longest, or those who donate large sum of money to the church). Let me show you some differences of how a corporation-structure type of church is different from a biblically based church.

Corporation Structure

1) One church with one elder

2) Elections based on popularity

3) Democratically elected

4) Distinction between ruling and teaching elders

5) Highest court appeals to man through a General Assembly

6) General Assembly oversees the whole church denomination

7) Human system of government

8) Leadership by one man

Biblical Structure

1) One church with several elders

2) Eldership appoints based on leadership skills

3) Theocratically appointed

4) No distinction: All elders rule and teach

5) Highest court appeals to God; no General Assembly

6) The fivefold ministries oversee the whole church; no denomination

7) Divine order of government

8) Leadership by several people

Here is a chart that emphasizes how church should function.

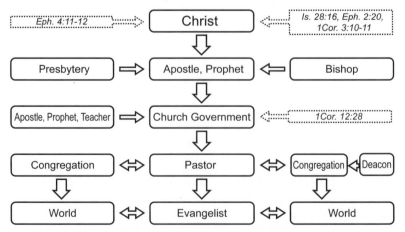

I have put together this chart based upon the New Testament. In the New Testament, *apostles* and *prophets* established and governed churches. *Pastors* did not establish or govern churches. Teachers also worked alongside the prophets (Acts 13:1). Apostles were sent out from the local church by the elders of that church (Acts 13:1–3). They were globally minded. The apostles cast lots and appointed another person to take Judas's place (Acts 1:15–26). The apostles appointed deacons because they were full of faith and of the Holy Spirit, not because they were popular or had been in the church the longest (Acts 6:5–7). The church in the book of Acts was a family because everyone had a giving spirit. No one person or people claimed anything as their own, but they distributed to each one in need (Acts 2:44–47; 4:32–34). We do not see this kind of giving in the churches today. Instead of giving, individual churches want to receive more. But in Acts, the church was focused on helping people, as one family member would help out another family member.

Now, God is restoring the true identity of the church by reestablishing apostles and prophets so that they can teach the church to become a "family-based business" rather than a "corporation." Under the corporation structure, the church lost all of God's power and they could not represent who He was. The church became a disability institute because many people were getting hurt, especially by not knowing who they were or their destiny. The church did not know that she had the anointing, and thus she ended up confusing the people.

Relationships

God is restoring our identity through building relationships rather than denominations. Relationships are more effective because they are more personal. Identity comes through relating with someone who can lead us to our destiny. That's why, these days, the Spirit of God is restoring the father-son relationships in the church.

Behold, I will send you Elijah the prophet
Before the coming of the great and dreadful day of the
LORD.
And he will turn
The hearts of the fathers to the children,
And the hearts of the children to their fathers,
Lest I come and strike the earth with a curse.
MAL. 4:5–6

God is preparing His servants in these days to bring a radical change about in the church. We have been playing church all these years, and now we need to stop pretending and start living out our destiny. Many people have made going to church a routine, but this routine gave people nothing to look forward when they went to church. God is doing something new to stir up the people in the church. This something new is called the "new wineskin." The new wineskin is a structural change in the life of the church. As a result, the church will not be controlled by a hierarchy or a denomination, but it will function through relationships, where the foundation needs to be properly built.

You are...fellow citizens with the saints and members of
*the household of God, having been **built on the founda-***
tion of the apostles and prophets, Jesus Christ Himself
being the chief cornerstone, in whom the whole building,
***being fitted together,** grows into a holy temple in the Lord.*
EPH. 2:19–21, EMPHASIS MINE

Tradition

The church has been following traditions that have limited the work of God. Many people in the church fear change and do not want to take any risks. Tradition makes people feel comfortable with what they are doing, because what they are doing was successful in the past or because the church has been doing it for years. Basically, these people are afraid of one word: *change.* Being traditional will not allow someone or something to bring about change. *Change* is a scary word because it requires something that is not stable. It requires risk. Change requires things to be restructured, and that is not what tradition wants, because tradition wants to keep things as they are. Tradition is predictable, but predictability will quench the flow of the Spirit because it has a set order. It will never be able to open to any new moves of the Spirit. Predictability brings limitations. Predictability does the same things again and again, hoping for different results each time. This kind of mentality will not advance the church, but will take it farther away from where God wants them to be. The church often wants to commit to what is safe, to "be on the safe side." I am not condemning tradition, but what I am saying is that there needs to be a time for change because certain things can't work forever. Each generation has its own form of bringing the Kingdom of God into the earth without compromising the Gospel.

Restoration of the Fivefold Ministry

Until the church restores the fivefold ministry gifts to the church, she will still continue to struggle and lack the anointing of God. The church needs to restore apostles and prophets for several reasons:

1) **To reproduce sons and daughters in the faith who will continue to work for the Kingdom**.

What the church lacks are spiritual fathers, who will guide future leaders. Spiritual fathers bring direction and stability.

> *For though you might have ten thousand instructors in Christ, **yet you do not have many fathers**, for in Christ Jesus I have begotten you through the gospel. Therefore I urge you, imitate me.*
> 1 COR. 4:15–16, EMPHASIS MINE

People can't only learn from information. They also need to learn through firsthand experience. Firsthand experience places us on the frontlines. Firsthand experience is a valuable resource because it teaches us about our mistakes in life, through trial and error. The way we succeed is by learning from our mistakes.

Another reason that apostles and prophets must be restored back in the church is:

2) To equip the saints for the work of the ministry and for the edification of the body.

> *And He Himself gave some to be apostles, some prophets, some evangelists, and some pastors and teachers, **for the equipping of the saints for the work of ministry, for the edifying of the body of Christ,** till we all come to the unity of the faith and of the knowledge of the Son of God, to a perfect man, to the measure of the stature of the fullness of Christ.*
> EPH. 4:11–13, EMPHASIS MINE

Apostles and prophets are the missing pieces that the church needs in order to become fully mature and also to be united in faith. Along with the other three offices, they work together for the common good of the people. It is all based upon teamwork to equip the saints, to prepare them for the work of ministry and to edify the body of Christ.

Through the years, evangelists, pastors, and teachers have been recognized in the body of Christ, but we tend to forget about apostles and prophets. Some have even argued that these offices stopped when the last apostle and prophet died. If we say someone is an apostle, some may think that they have the authority to add to Scripture, but that is not what the Bible teaches. These two ministry gifts have to be restored back to the church in order for us to reach unity and maturity in the faith. I will not expand more about apostles and prophets here. I just want to explain that these two ministry gifts are very essential to the body of Christ, and they need to be restored in order for the church to walk in the full anointing of God.

The final reason for the restoration of apostles and prophets in the church is:

3) To cause the church to be relational rather than denominational.

When Jesus came to the earth, He maintained a consistent relationship with the Father. He communicated with the Father. And as they communicated, the Father empowered the Son. Churches need to be relational because denominations alone can't impart the life and power of the Lord.

> *Then Jesus answered and said to them, "Most assuredly, I say to you, the Son can do nothing of Himself, but what He sees the Father do; for whatever He does, the Son also does in like manner. For the Father loves the Son, and shows Him all things that He Himself does; and He will show Him greater works than these, that you may marvel."*
>
> JOHN 5:19–20

This passage demonstrates the close relationship between the Father and the Son. We need to focus on how strong the relationship between the Father and the Son actually was. Everything the Father did, the Son did it in like manner. The Father gave all the authority to the Son to carry out His mission.

Their relationship also shows that the Son was in total submission to the will of the Father. The strong bond they had is what imparted to the Son everything that the Father had. Jesus came to reproduce who He was in the lives of His twelve apostles. The church needs to reproduce sons and daughters so that those sons and daughters can then reproduce other sons and daughters, and so advance the Gospel.

CHAPTER FIVE

Accountability

A Family Business

God wants the church to be more like a family than a corporation. Every church needs to have a relationship with an apostle. In the Scriptures, the apostles were men chosen by God to lead the church. They were given this authority from the Lord. One example is found in Acts 5, when Ananias and Sapphira kept back some of the money they had pledged to the church. God used the apostles to bring judgment for their foolish act. Apostles make sure that the church is functioning properly. The fivefold ministry that God originally designed must be restored for the church to function properly and fulfill her destiny. Apostles reveal the church's identity and help her to walk toward her destiny. They provide strategies on how the local church can win its particular geographical location for the Lord.

With this type of structure in place, the church will come to realize her full potential in the Lord and receive the anointing of God to fulfill her main purpose. The church must be relational if it is to impart the heart of God to the people. If the church is based upon relationships, it will carry with it the heart of God, because the church will be one. And when the church is one, it can then go out into the world and share the love of God with others.

Relationships are effective because they are personal. Their effectiveness lies in the fact that personal relationships deal with the heart. Our hearts determine if we will open ourselves up to people and build an intimate relationship based on encouragement, accountability, and strength. This heart issue also deals with integrity, another important issue. Men and women of God must be filled with integrity, for integrity is one of the key components of building relationships. Integrity will keep a relationship close.

The Upcoming Younger Generation of Ministers

Issues of the heart are especially important for young people who feel called to the ministry. When young people are called by God, they usually then go through years of seminary training, but unfortunately when they leave the seminary, they have a hard time doing actual ministry. This is because they have no father-like figure to speak into their lives and impart the anointing of God upon their lives. Apostles not only teach head knowledge, but they also teach by demonstration. Young people who are called into the ministry need to have someone to share their experiences, someone to show them firsthand how to do ministry. That's why Paul wrote these words to the Corinthians:

> *Therefore I urge you, imitate me.*
> 1 COR. 4:16

Paul also had a close relationship with Timothy. When Paul thought Timothy was ready, he sent him out to start his own ministry. Paul spent time showing Timothy what ministry was all about, and when the time came, he sent him out on his own. But he didn't abandon Timothy. He wrote the Pastoral Epistles (1 and 2 Timothy and Titus) to instruct Timothy on how to appoint elders and how to set things in order. He also warned about false teachers and doctrines that would deceive many in the last days.

The Roles of Spiritual Fathers

Within a family structure, both parents are very important to a child's development. Although I am expanding on the roles of fathers in this section, I in no way mean to diminish the role of the mother. Each parent brings something of great importance to a child.

Fathers are critical to a child's identity; they speak into their children's lives to give them a sense of worth and purpose. In other words, they give them "direction." Fathers reveal and affirm to their children who they are, why they were born (their purpose), and where they are going. Fathers show their children that they are accepted and loved for who they are. They help their children to become future leaders.

> *And suddenly a voice came from heaven, saying, "This is*
> *My beloved Son, in whom I am well pleased."*
> MATT. 3:17

God revealed that He was well pleased with Jesus before His mission even began. Fathers should be pleased with their children before they ever accomplish anything. This acceptance will strengthen the child's life and cause them to strive to reach their full potential.

Concerning ministry, young people need spiritual fathers to help them find their direction and to fulfill their purpose for the Kingdom of God. Fathers remind their sons and daughters of the true nature of their identity and that God wants to fulfill His purpose through them. In ministry, there are certain things that only fathers can impart to their sons and daughters by speaking to them on a personal level.

Fathers also reproduce themselves—who they are. They carry the seed that is necessary for the next generation to prosper and succeed. Fathers impart to their children what they themselves have received from the Lord. This impartation is a blessing that God bestows upon the children to faithfully carry out the work of God. Fathers give their children the spiritual life that propels them to birth new life. Fathers want to see their children succeed, excel, and do better than what they themselves were able to do.

The Double Portion

Fathers leave something behind for their children. Fathers train their spiritual children so that they can "take over the family business." This is called an "inheritance." There is not only a worldly inheritance, but there is a spiritual one as well. In the natural world, after a father dies, the children receive the inheritance. This occurs when the father has worked hard all his life, and he passes it down to his children, so that they can continue the family business. In a spiritual relationship, the inheritance comes in a spiritual sense. This is often called the "double portion." The double portion allows us to do great things for God.

> Jesus said, "Most assuredly, I say to you, he who believes in Me, **the works that I do he will do also; and greater works than these he will do,** because I go to My Father."
> JOHN 14:12, EMPHASIS MINE

Moscow

The Lord allowed many miracles to be associated with my ministry to Moscow. I held a special outreach Christian concert for non-believers. As I was approaching the stage to make my greeting, the Lord gave me a word of knowledge that there was a woman who was being attacked by the spirit of suicide. I spoke to the audience, asking the woman to come up to the front so that I could pray for her. She stood up and came forward, and the Lord led me to pray for her and to give her a word of encouragement. As I spoke, I sensed that the Spirit was working inside of her, and that evening, she was totally delivered from the spirit of suicide. She had planned to commit suicide that evening, and so, through the concert, the Lord saved her life.

I also saw the blind healed in St. Petersburg. There was a young man there in his twenties who had been born with open eyes, but without vision. At that time, I had four prayer teams with me to pray for the massive numbers of people who were seeking healing. Although the blind man went to all four prayer teams for healing, he still remained blind. Finally, he came up to me and told me that he had gone to each prayer team with no success. He came up to me by faith and asked for prayer. As I prayed, I witnessed a miracle. The man was healed from his blindness right then, as I prayed for him.

Another interesting miracle occurred when I was speaking at a service and a woman approached me with bread in her hands. She explained that this bread was for her husband, who was not a Christian. She wanted me to pray for her husband to receive salvation, but she asked me to pray for the bread—that when he ate it, he would be saved. I prayed for her and the bread. The following day, the same woman came to the service, but this time, she came with her husband. They both explained to me that as he ate that bread, something happened to him, and he received the Lord as His Savior. Hallelujah!

The double portion allows us to do greater things than what our spiritual fathers did. This is the inheritance that is gained through a covenant spiritual relationship between a father and his spiritual children. Sons and daughters serve their fathers and receive double, or even more than double, of what their fathers were given. Do you believe that you can do great things for the Lord? The Scripture says that we can do greater things than what the Lord Jesus did Himself. What kinds of "greater things" can we do that Jesus did not do while He was on the earth? When Jesus went back to heaven, He did not leave us powerless. He sent us the Holy Spirit.

A Dead Man Raised in a Restaurant

In early 1990, I attended an apostolic and prophetic conference in Frederick, Maryland. One day, I ate lunch with another minister and two other women at a Chinese restaurant in a small shopping center. While we were talking, the Holy Spirit spoke to me and asked me to turn my head. When I turned my head, I saw a man with his head lying flat on the table. The Lord specifically told me that he had died from a heart attack, and He then asked me to go pray for him. Praying for a dead person is difficult because there seems to be no solution. But I obeyed what the Lord told me to do and went over to the man. When I lifted his head, I saw that he was indeed dead. I got the courage to make an announcement to those at the restaurant, stating to everyone that I was a minister and that the man with his head on the table was dead. Everyone in the restaurant was shocked and couldn't believe it. The owner of the restaurant, especially, was very nervous and upset that there was a dead person in his restaurant, and he decided to call for an ambulance.

One of the ladies with us was a registered nurse, and at that time, she examined the man and confirmed that he was indeed dead. I asked the people in the restaurant to stay where they were, and I then called my minister friend over, asking him to pray with me for this person. I knew that God wanted to restore this man back to life, and so I just proclaimed a simple prayer, asking that " In the name of Jesus!, I bind the spirit of death, I loose the spirit of life would return to this body". As soon as I prayed, the man lifted up his head—he was alive! Everyone at the restaurant was shocked. When the ambulance finally came, they could not find anything wrong with the man. The paramedics decided to take him to the hospital for an examination, just in case. My friends and I followed the ambulance to the hospital. When we saw the doctor, he said that the man was completely normal. I later learned that he had indeed suffered from a heart failure or attack—but that he was fine.

These are some of many ways that the Lord has used me to do great works for Him. Do we have the power to raise the dead? Do we have the power to heal the blind? Could this be what the Lord meant when He said that we would do greater works than Him? We should not put God in a box and limit His ability to move in our lives. He can do anything and use anyone for His purpose. We just need to be open to be used by Him.

The Keys to Receiving the Double Portion

How can we receive this double portion? The double portion does not come automatically. We can see this through the lives of Elijah and Elisha. Elisha received the double portion, simply because he was Elijah's son and served him.

> [We desire] that you do not become sluggish, but imitate those who through faith and patience inherit the promises.
> HEB. 6:12

The inheritance is something you receive, not something you need to work for. The inheritance comes through relationship. Elijah went through many times of rejection, testing, hardships, and trials to become a powerful man of God. Elisha, on the other hand, was in a submitted relationship with Elijah, following and serving him. Through that submission, he received the double portion. This is such a wonderful blessing to have. Because Elisha was a faithful son, he received the double portion. Faithful submission to a spiritual father brings rich blessings: As Jesus submitted to the will of God, He demonstrated the heart of a faithful son. Elisha had the same attitude, even calling Elijah his father just after he was taken to heaven.

> *And Elisha saw it, and he cried out, "**My father, my father.**"*
> 2 KINGS 2:12

There are several keys to receiving the double portion. The first key is:

a) A Commitment/Covenant Relationship

Without a true commitment to your spiritual father, you can't receive the double portion. We can't compromise if we are to receive the double portion. In the New Testament, there was to be no compromise if you wanted to follow Jesus.

> *Then Jesus said to His disciples, "If anyone desires to come after Me, let him deny himself, and take up his cross, and follow Me. For whoever desires to save his life will lose it, but whoever loses his life for My sake will find it."*
> MATT. 16:24–25

We need to be committed in order to see the double portion come upon our life. We can't give up, no matter what happens.

> *And so it was, when they had crossed over, that Elijah said to Elisha, "Ask! What may I do for you, before I am taken away from you?" Elisha said, "Please let a double portion of your spirit be upon me." So he said, "You have asked a hard thing. Nevertheless, if you see me when I am taken from you, it shall be so for you; but if not, it shall not be so.... And Elisha saw it, and he cried out."*
> 2 KINGS 2:9–10, 12

We need to die to our own visions, placing our own agendas on the cross, and serve our father's vision. Being committed means that we do this, even if we have to start from scratch. Elisha was willing to be a water boy for Elijah. He was willing to carry his books and his bags, serve him food, and care for his needs. This time of service was also a time for Elisha to grow in character and in integrity. He became willing to do even the meaningless tasks, just so that he could serve. Elisha was willing, and his attitude showed his commitment.

Being in a covenant relationship also means that spiritual "children" should pay their tithes to their spiritual "fathers." Fathers are the storehouses to whom we should pay our tithes. Many Christians misunderstand the true meaning of the word *storehouse*. The word *storehouse* in the Hebrew language means "distributor; builder; house builder; or stewardship." Unfortunately, many Christians believe that church is a building where we all gather to meet. And because they meet in a building, they believe they should pay their tithes to the church. However, the church is actually the people—not a building. The people who are gathered together comprise the church. Where should we bring our tithes when the church is not a building but people?

This is one fact that we need to understand: The congregation of the church should tithe to the spiritual leader or overseer of their church; however, the spiritual leader or overseer should not tithe to their own church! Instead, they should tithe to their spiritual covering, their own spiritual fathers. The way that people have been tithing is unbiblical. Pastors and overseers have been tithing to their own churches. The church supports the pastor and the overseer, so, the pastor or overseer of the church has basically been tithing to himself. This is not scriptural! Storehouses are meant to be distributors. Spiritual fathers are the storehouses. Just as the pastor or overseer of the church is a distributor to the congregation, the spiritual father is the distributor to the pastor or overseer.

We need to understand that the spiritual leader, or father, leads the Christian community of the church. He is the one who brings covering over the people. In the Old Testament, the people brought their tithes to the priest (Gen. 28:22; Num. 18:21–28; Deut. 12:5–9, 11–12, 17–18; 14:22–28; 26:1–14; 1 Sam. 8:15–17; 2 Chron. 31:5–11; Neh. 10:37–38; 12:44; 13:5, 12). Also, in the New Testament, we see that it is the new covenant (Matt. 26:26–29). In the book of Acts, after the people sold their possessions, they brought their money, and laid it at the apostles' feet (Acts 4:35, 37). The apostles were their spiritual fathers.

We can also see this through the Last Supper Jesus had with His disciples. Jesus provided bread and wine to His disciples. Tithe was before Moses' Law . (Gen 14:20). Tithing is not a commandment in Moses' Law, but it is a covenant between God and us. That's why the Old Testament is a foreshadowing of the New (Acts 4:32–37; Heb. 7:5–9).

Spiritual fathers are the distributors in their children's life. We always thought that we were to pay our tithes to the church. Well, spiritual children are to pay their tithes to their spiritual fathers because these are the ones who cover their ministries.

> "Bring all the tithes into the storehouse,
> *That there may be food in My house,*
> *And try Me now in this,"*
> *Says the LORD of hosts.*
> MAL. 3:10

> *[Melchizedek king of Salem said:] "Blessed be God Most High,*
> *Who has delivered your enemies into your hand."*
> *And he gave him tithe of all.*
> GEN. 14:20

Abram gave a tenth of what he had to King Melchizedek because Melchizedek had given bread and wine to Abram. Spiritual fathers bring bread and wine to their children. This then leads the children to tithe, to give a tenth of their income to their fathers.

The Bible talks about honoring our parents, but how are we to do that? When the Bible talks about honoring our parents, it is always connected with material goods. Scripture talks about honoring God. We honor God through our possessions.

> *Honor the Lord with your possessions,*
> *And with the firstfruits of all your increase.*
> Prov. 3:9

Because we honor God with our possessions, we honor our parents through the same means. Because our spiritual fathers are also our spiritual guardians, we should honor them by tithing and offering to them.

The next key to receiving the double portion is:

b) Chasing Your Spiritual Father

Elisha followed Elijah wherever he went. Even when Elijah told Elisha to stay behind, he still insisted on following:

> *Then Elijah said to Elisha, "Stay here, please, for the Lord has sent me on to Bethel." But Elisha said, "As the Lord lives, and as your soul lives, I will not leave you!" So they went down to Bethel. Now the sons of the prophets who were at Bethel came out to Elisha, and said to him, "Do you know that the Lord will take away your master from over you today?" And he said, "Yes, I know; keep silent!" Then Elijah said to him, "Elisha, stay here, please, for the Lord has sent me on to Jericho." But he said, "As the Lord lives, and as your soul lives, I will not leave you!" So they came to Jericho. Now the sons of the prophets who were at Jericho came to Elisha and said to him, "Do you know that the Lord will take away your master from over you today?" So he answered, "Yes, I*

know; keep silent!" Then Elijah said to him, "Stay here,
please, for the LORD has sent me on to the Jordan." But he
said, "As the LORD lives, and as your soul lives, I will not
leave you!" So the two of them went on.
2 KINGS 2:2–6

We must be ready to follow our fathers wherever they go. Elisha kept on pursuing Elijah. He did not let go of what he had committed to. In a Hebrew context, it would mean something like this: If a puppy bites down on a blanket, and you want the blanket back, you may try to pull it away from the dog. That puppy will not let go without a fight! In order to receive the double portion, we need to have the same nature as that puppy with its hold on the blanket. We need to chase our spiritual father with this same attitude, or we will not experience the supernatural things in our life.

The third key to receiving the double portion is:

c) Tearing Your Own Mantle into Two Pieces

When Elijah was taken up to heaven, Elisha had to tear his own mantle before he could put on Elijah's.

And he took hold of his own clothes and tore them into
two pieces.
2 KINGS 2:12

When we symbolically tear our own mantle, we are taking over for what our father worked so hard. We can't have our own agendas or plans. We must be willing to leave everything and follow our father's work. It is hard to just drop everything and try to adjust to someone else's plan, making it our own. That's why, in order to receive the double portion, there needs to be a sacrifice, or a willingness to pay the price.

The final key to receiving the double portion is:

d) Picking Up and Wearing Your Father's Mantle

When Elijah was gone, Elisha saw his leader's mantle on the floor. And after he tore his own, he picked up Elijah's mantle and put it on himself.

> *He also took up the mantle of Elijah that had fallen from him, and went back and stood by the bank of the Jordan. Then he took the mantle of Elijah that had fallen from him, and struck the water.*
> 2 KINGS 2:13–14

We can't put our fathers' mantle on over our own mantles. The double portion is received when our own vision and agenda is dropped and we continue our father's vision.

Elijah and Elisha

We can learn many things about a father-son relationship through the lives of Elijah and Elisha. Elijah was like a father to Elisha. Everywhere that Elijah went, Elisha followed. He did not want to leave the presence of his father. He served his father with joy and commitment. He was even willing to do meaningless tasks for his father. His main objective in life was to be where his father was.

> *Then he arose and followed Elijah, and became his servant.*
> 1 KINGS 19:21

This type of relationship is similar to that of Jesus and His disciples. The disciples went with Him wherever He went and saw how He ministered to the people. Jesus is a type of Elijah, and we are a type of Elisha.

We need to know our spiritual father, especially what he is doing. Elisha always knew what Elijah was doing. The best students always know what their master is doing. When the fifty sons of the prophets asked if Elisha knew that God was going to take Elijah away, he responded that he did, in fact, know that.

> *Now the sons of the prophets who were at Jericho came to Elisha and said to him, "Do you know that the LORD will take away your master from over you today?" So he answered, "Yes, I know; keep silent!"*
> 2 KINGS 2:5

Fathers are concerned about the needs of their children. Spiritual fathers know that their children need double of what they have been given in order to continue. Without a spiritual father, we will be alone in this world.

CHAPTER SIX

Christ–The Image of God

The Anointing

When God created us, He created us in His image. Many Christians do not understand what this means. We have never thought about what the true image of God really is. The Bible says that Christ is the image of God.

> *Even if our gospel is veiled, it is veiled to those who are perishing, whose minds the god of this age has blinded, who do not believe, lest the light of the gospel of the glory of **Christ, who is the image of God**, should shine on them.*
> 2 COR. 4:4, EMPHASIS MINE

When we were created in His image, we were given power and the authority of heaven over the earth. God created man to be like Christ. The anointing inside of us crucifies our lives on the cross so that we can be more like Jesus Christ. Without the anointing in our lives, we will not be able to crucify our lives daily. That's why Christ lives in us.

> *I have been crucified with Christ; it is no longer I who*
> *live, but* **Christ lives in me**; *and the life which I now live*
> *in the flesh I live by faith in the Son of God, who loved*
> *me and gave Himself for me.*
> GAL. 2:20, EMPHASIS MINE

To say that Christ lives in us really means that the anointing lives in us. But if we do not die to our old nature, we will lack the anointing in our lives. And when that happens, we will walk in the flesh.

The Bible clearly says that we have an anointing, and that through this, we should be able to discern everything.

> *But* **you have an anointing from the Holy One** *and* **you**
> **know all things**.
> 1 JOHN 2:20, EMPHASIS MINE

We have the ability to discern the Spirit of God, the devil, and even mankind. When we have the anointing of God, we will be able to abide with God. We will be able to hear everything He says.

> *The anointing which you have received from Him abides*
> *in you,* *and you do not need that anyone teach you; but*
> *as the same anointing teaches you concerning all things,*
> *and is true, and is not a lie, and just as it has taught you,*
> *you will abide in Him.*
> 1 JOHN 2:27, EMPHASIS MINE

Because we abide with God through the anointing, we will be able to discern the three types of spirits: the Holy Spirit, evil spirits, and the spirit of man. We need the anointing in our life more than ever before. Because the world is growing darker, we need to have the anointing more abundantly. The Bible says that we can do all things in Christ.

> *I can do all things* **through Christ** *who strengthens me.*
> PHIL. 4:13, EMPHASIS MINE

To be "in Christ" means to be in the anointing. The anointing helps us to do and accomplish all things in life.

What is this anointing that we have? Is it crucial that we know and understand the anointing. To *anoint* means "to consecrate, or make sacred." The word *anointing* means to be covered or smeared with oil. Our lives must be covered by the Holy Spirit. The anointing inside of us is what separates us from the world. It empowers us and gives us the wisdom that we need to deliver people from bondage.

> *There shall come forth a Rod from the stem of Jesse,*
> *And a Branch shall grow out of his roots.*
> *The Spirit of the* Lord *shall rest upon Him,*
> *The Spirit of wisdom and understanding,*
> *The Spirit of counsel and might,*
> The Spirit of knowledge and of the fear of the Lord.
> Isa. 11:1–2

Basically, this anointing that we have is the power of God.
> **Christ [is] the power of God** *and the wisdom of God.*
> 1 Cor. 1:24, emphasis mine

God has also given us the spirit of power.

> *God has not given us a spirit of fear, but of power and of love and of a sound mind.*
> 2 Tim. 1:7

This is why we should know everything, especially what is going on in life. Due to our lack of understanding of the anointing, we always seem to be struggling to find our purpose in life.

The anointing helps us to be transformed from glory to glory. Christ is the glory of God.

> *But we all, with unveiled face, beholding as in a mirror the glory of the Lord, are being transformed **into the same image from glory to glory**, just as by the Spirit of the Lord.*
> 2 Cor. 3:18, emphasis mine

The Mystery of the Indwelling Christ

We are always in a process of transformation. We are being changed to the image of God, which is Christ every day. In Christ, God is changing you into His image, restoring back all the authority and power that was lost in the Garden of Eden. This is the concept of the "mystery of Christ." What is the mystery of the indwelling Christ? First of all, the mystery of God is in Christ.

> *I now rejoice in my sufferings for you, and fill up in my flesh what is lacking in the afflictions of Christ, for the sake of His body, which is the church, of which I became a minister according to the stewardship from God which was given to me for you, to fulfill the word of God, **the mystery which has been hidden** from ages and from generations, but now has been revealed to His saints. To them God willed it to make known what are the riches of the glory of this mystery among the Gentiles: which is **Christ in you, the hope of glory**.*
> COL. 1:24–27, EMPHASIS MINE

Next, the mystery of Christ is the Godhead incarnate in Him, in whom every believer is complete.

> *...that their hearts may be encouraged, being knit together in love, and attaining to all riches of the full assurance of understanding, to the knowledge of the mystery of God, both of the Father and of Christ, in whom are hidden all the treasures of wisdom and knowledge.... For **in Him dwells all the fullness of the Godhead bodily; and you are complete in Him**, who is the head of all principality and power.*
> COL. 2:2–3, 9–10, EMPHASIS MINE

Thirdly, the mystery of Christ is the church, a mystery hidden from past ages.

*By revelation He made known to me the mystery (as I have briefly written already, by which, when you read, you may understand my knowledge in the mystery of Christ), which in other ages was not made known to the sons of men, as it has now been revealed by the Spirit to His holy apostles and prophets: that the Gentiles should be fellow heirs, of the same body, and partakers of His promise in Christ through the gospel, of which I became a minister according to the gift of the grace of God given to me by the effective working of His power. To me, who am less than the least of all the saints, this grace was given, that I should preach among the Gentiles the unsearchable riches of Christ, and to make all see what is the fellowship of **the mystery, which from the beginning of the ages has been hidden in God who created all things through Jesus Christ; to the intent that now the manifold wisdom of God might be made known by the church to the principalities and powers in the heavenly places,** according to the eternal purpose which He accomplished in Christ Jesus our Lord.*

EPH. 3:3–11, EMPHASIS MINE

Finally, the mystery of God is the bride of Christ. The married life of a Spirit-filled believer illustrates the relationship between Christ and His church.

Wives, submit to your own husbands, as to the Lord. For the husband is head of the wife, as also Christ is head of the church; and He is the Savior of the body. Therefore, just as the church is subject to Christ, so let the wives be to their own husbands in everything. Husbands, love your wives, just as Christ also loved the church and gave Himself for her, that He might sanctify and cleanse her with the washing of water by the word, that He might present her to Himself a glorious church, not having spot or wrinkle or any such thing, but that she should be holy and without blemish. So husbands ought to love their own wives as their own bodies; he who loves his wife loves himself. For no one ever hated his own flesh, but *nourishes and cherishes it, just as the Lord does the church. For we are members of His body, of His flesh and of His bones. "For this reason a man shall leave his father and mother and be joined to his wife, and the two shall become one flesh." **This is a great mystery, but I speak concerning Christ and the church.** Nevertheless let each one of you in particular so love his own wife as himself, and let the wife see that she respects her husband.*

EPH. 5:22–33, EMPHASIS MINE

If you are not being transformed daily, you are not constantly becoming a new creation. Our old lifestyle must constantly be changed.

Therefore, if anyone is in Christ, he is a new creation; old things have passed away; behold, all things have become new.

2 COR. 5:17

If we know who Christ is, then our lives will be changed. The reason why our lives have not yet changed is that we have been focusing on the past. Being a new creation means that the past is history. Your old lifestyle will not determine your destiny in the Lord because you are a new creation in Christ. God wants to bring you into a new dimension.

This new dimension gives us excitement, because we are always waiting to see how God will move in our lives. We complain because the way of the Lord is not comfortable to us. We don't realize how we got saved. If we realize how we got saved, we would always be thanking Him instead of complaining to Him.

How can we trust the Lord? If you don't understand the image of God, the person of God, and the anointing of God, you will never know God Himself or trust anything that He says. As believers, we sometimes can't trust the Lord. Why is that? It is because we do not know the Holy Spirit, who also is the Person of God. Who is inside of us? It is Christ. Christ is the image of the invisible God.

He is the image of the invisible God, the firstborn over all creation.
CoL. 1:15

All things were created by Him. So, the Creator is inside of us.

[The Israelites] of whom are the fathers and from whom, according to the flesh, Christ came, who is over all, the eternally blessed God. Amen.
Rom. 9:5

Christ is over the entire heaven and earth. He is the blessed eternal God. He moves wherever we move.

"You are sons of the prophets, and of the covenant which God made with our fathers, saying to Abraham, 'And in **your seed all the families of the earth shall be blessed'***. To you first, God, having raised up His Servant Jesus, sent Him to bless you, in turning away every one of you from your iniquities."*
Acts 3:25–26, emphasis mine

This is a promise to which we can hold. We are the resource of blessing on this earth. Because Christ is in us, the anointing goes with us wherever we go. Now, what kind of promise was given? We need to take a look at the promise given to Abraham. First, who is Abraham's seed? Christ is the seed of Abraham.

For you are all sons of God through faith in Christ Jesus. For as many of you as were baptized into Christ have put on Christ. There is neither Jew nor Greek, there is neither slave nor free, there is neither male nor female; for you are all one in Christ Jesus. **And if you are Christ's, then you are Abraham's seed, and heirs according to the promise***.*
Gal. 3:26–29, emphasis mine

What kind of promise have we been given? We need to look at another passage of scripture. We need to look at Abraham's calling in order to understand the promise.

> Now the LORD had said to Abram:
> "Get out of your country,
> From your family
> And from your father's house,
> To a land that I will show you.
> I will make you a great nation;
> I will bless you
> **And make your name great;**
> And **you shall be a blessing.**
> I will bless those who bless you,
> And I will curse him who curses you,
> **And in you all the families of the earth shall be blessed.**"
> GEN. 12:1–3, EMPHASIS MINE

If you want to get a blessing from the Lord, the first thing you must do is to leave your family, your land, and your father's house. This passage is not talking about your natural family. It is talking about those to whom you belonged before you turned to Jesus. Ephesians 2 tells us that our forefather is Satan. You must leave your forefather and the land of curses and travel to the promised land. If you don't, you will not inherit the blessing.

God has given us a great blessing. We need to believe in His promise. The Word of God tells us that it will accomplish whatever we say.

> So shall My word be that goes forth from My mouth;
> It shall not return to Me void,
> **But it shall accomplish** what I please,
> And it shall prosper in the thing for which I sent it.
> ISA. 55:11, EMPHASIS MINE

If you do not know who Christ is, and if you don't live in the anointing of God, you are still under a curse.

*For as many as are of the works of the law are under the curse; for it is written, "Cursed is everyone who does not continue in all things which are written in the book of the law, to do them." But that no one is justified by the law in the sight of God is evident, for "the just shall live by faith." Yet the law is not of faith but the man who does them shall live by them. Christ has redeemed us from the curse of the law, having become a curse for us (**for it is written, "Cursed is everyone who hangs on a tree"**), that the blessing of Abraham might come upon the Gentiles in Christ Jesus, that we might receive the promise of the Spirit through faith. Brethren, I speak in the manner of men: Though it is only a man's covenant, yet if it is confirmed, no one annuls or adds to it. Now to Abraham and his Seed were the promises made. He does not say, "And to seeds," as of many, but as of one, "And to your Seed," who is Christ. And this I say, that the law, which was four hundred and thirty years later, cannot annul the covenant that was confirmed before by God in Christ, that it should make the promise of no effect. For if the inheritance is of the law, it is no longer of promise; but God gave it to Abraham by promise.*

GAL. 3:10–18, EMPHASIS MINE

The curse was broken in Christ. This passage says that whoever hangs on the tree is cursed. Jesus hung on the tree. He became a curse for us. But if you don't hang on the tree with Jesus, the curse is still remaining upon your life. If we really comprehend who Christ is, the curse will be forever removed from us. Christ is the anointed one of God. If you are under the anointing of God, you are not under the curse, but you are under grace. We need the power of the Holy Spirit upon our life. If we don't flow with the Spirit, the curse will try to attack us.

It shall come to pass in that day
That his burden will be taken away from your shoulder,
And his yoke from your neck,

*And **the yoke will be destroyed because of the anointing oil**.*

ISA. 10:27, EMPHASIS MINE

This is the anointing that breaks the yoke of the enemy. The anointing inside of us gives us the authority to carry out the tasks that have been given to us. That is why we need the anointing of God. We need to believe that He who is in us is greater than he who is in this earth.

*You are of God, little children, and have overcome them, because **He who is in you is greater than he who is in the world***

1 JOHN 4:4, EMPHASIS MINE

The word *salvation* in the Greek language can be translated as *sozo* and *soteria*. These words do not only mean that we have a one-way ticket to heaven. The word *sozo* includes the prosperity of our spirits, souls, and bodies. When we were saved, we not only received eternal life for the future, but we also received benefits here for the present. God restored physical health and prosperity along with His power and authority.

The apostle Paul confessed that he needed to die daily. Why did he need to die daily? So that everything that was old in his life would be totally gone. He couldn't allow anything to be attached to his life that would hinder him from living a purpose-driven life for the Lord. He considered the anointing as something precious in his life.

Adam was to worship God and protect the Garden of Eden. That was his responsibility. But once he was deceived, he lost that authority and a curse fell upon mankind. This happened because Adam did not protect what was inside of him. We need to protect the anointing inside of us. How much do you value the anointing inside of you? We must value the anointing because it is the key to everything. It breaks bondages, teaches us God's truth, and gives us the dominion as Christians. The anointing always abides with us.

Baptism in the Holy Spirit

God baptizes us with the Holy Spirit. When that takes place, He gives us a global mindset, a mindset in which we focus on the entire world. God wants to send us across the world to continue what He started. The Bible states that "the whole world belongs to us."

> *He worked [His mighty power] in Christ when He raised Him from the dead and seated Him at His right hand in the heavenly places, far above all principality and power and might and dominion, and every name that is named, not only in this age but also in that which is to come. **And He put all things under His feet, and gave Him to be head over all things to the church***
> EPH. 1:20–22, EMPHASIS MINE

Before we can have the whole world, we must be crucified on the cross. When we are crucified with Christ, we become a new person. The crucifixion of our lives is very important to receive the anointing. This is how God wants to move us in a new direction. In what direction does God want to move us? He wants to move us toward the Promised Land.

God has given us a threefold anointing, and this threefold anointing is for one purpose. We need to understand why God brought the Hebrews out of Egypt. Why did God tell Moses to go back to Egypt? He wanted to deliver the people out of the darkness. God has called us to be deliverers of this world because this world is living in darkness. We are the true light that will bring liberty to people. When we are living like true deliverers, we are actually judging the world because we are bringing the world out of bondage.

CHAPTER SEVEN

The Threefold Anointing

Anointed Ones

We have a threefold anointing residing inside of us. In the Old Testament, the word *Messiah* meant "anointed one." But now, in Christ we have a threefold anointing:

> *...from Jesus Christ, the faithful witness, the firstborn from the dead, and the ruler over the kings of the earth. To Him who loved us and washed us from our sins in His own blood, and **has made us kings and priests** to His God and Father, to Him be glory and dominion forever and ever. Amen.*
>
> REV. 1:5–6, EMPHASIS MINE

This threefold anointing is related to three offices: the king, the priest, and the prophet. These three offices/anointings always work together. Government without stable direction will lead to corruption. If the church does not have direction and stability, it will be in chaos. Because we are in Christ, we have been given these anointings—for one purpose. We are to be judges in this dark world.

The Image of God

For the Lord *Most High is awesome;*
He is a great King over all the earth.
He will subdue the peoples under us
And the nations under our feet.
He will choose our inheritance for us,
The excellence of Jacob whom He loves.
Ps. 47:2–4

In this passage, God was speaking of the future church. These verses can be applied to the New Testament. If we are in Christ, He has made us as kings and priests. When God looks at us, He looks at what is inside of us, which is Jesus. Because Jesus is the King of the universe, we come from a royal heritage.

We are the true light of the world. This is the new direction to which God wants to bring us. Each of the offices of the three-fold anointing has a special function. In Scripture, each of these three offices judged the people of God. The Hebrew word for *judge* is *shapat.*, which means "to intercede; to be a mediator." It also means "to rule and reign as a king," or even "to give punishment." The judges were lawgivers. God is calling His church to be a lawgiver in this world. When we become lawgivers, we are executing God's laws.

Let the high praises of God be in their mouth,
And a two-edged sword in their hand,
To execute vengeance on the nations,
And punishments on the peoples;
To bind their kings with chains,
And their nobles with fetters of iron;
To execute on them the written judgment—
This honor have all His saints.
Praise the Lord.
Psalm 149:6–9

The Anointing of a King

First, the Bible says that we are all kings.

> [He] has **made us kings** and priests to His God and Father.
>
> REV. 1:6, EMPHASIS MINE

The Hebrew word for *king* is *melech*. We can see this through King Melchizedek:

> For this Melchizedek, king of Salem, priest of the Most High God, who met Abraham returning from the slaughter of the kings and blessed him, to whom also Abraham gave a tenth part of all, first being translated "king of righteousness," and then also king of Salem, meaning "king of peace," without father, without mother, without genealogy, having neither beginning of days nor end of life, but made like the Son of God, remains a priest continually.
>
> HEB. 7:1–3

The Old Testament demonstrates three different models of a king: King Saul, King David, and King Solomon. King Saul did not have a heart for God at all. We read that King Saul had an unstable faith (1 Sam. 13). One incident was when the Israelites were hard-pressed against the Philistines. The Philistines surrounded the Israelites and the people were very afraid of their presence. Now, the prophet Samuel told King Saul to wait for him seven days till he comes where he is. Now on the seventh day, King Saul had waited but prophet Samuel did not show up. King Saul did not have any patience and offered up the burnt offering without the prophet with him. He did everything in a rush and according to the circumstance that he was in. As soon as he finished offering up the burnt offering, Samuel came to Saul. Samuel saw that Saul already offered up the burnt offering without him. Samuel rebuked Saul for his foolishness and then he prophesied that the kingdom would be given to someone else.

This foolishness had cost Saul to lose his destiny as a king. We see here that King Saul did not function in his calling. When he offered up the burnt offering, he offered it up functioning as a priest, which was not his calling. He missed his destiny because he did not function in his proper calling.

Next we read about King David. King David, on the other hand, had a full heart for God. He was a man after God's own heart. We know the story of King David(2 Sam.11-12). While he was walking on the roof of his palace one night, he saw a beautiful woman, Bathsheba, taking a bath. As he saw her, he inquired to find out who she was. As soon as he found out that it was one of his soldier's wives, he had a plan to obtain her. He got what he wanted when he sent Uriah the soldier into the front of a heavy battle, where the chances of him dying, was high. As soon as he married Bathsheba, God sent Nathan, a prophet, to speak to David. When David realized that he committed the sin of adultery and murder, he immediately repented of his sins. He knew that his relationship with the Lord was relevant to his success (Ps.51). As soon as he repented, David continued to exercise his function as a king, with the consequences of his actions.

Lastly, we read about King Solomon. He started having a full heart for the Lord. He was blessed by having wisdom and understanding of the ways of the Lord. However, since he had many wives his heart started to be divided. He married into families with many foreign gods. He ended having a divided heart for God. His weakness was women and that caused him to bring in many foreign gods that hindered his reign as a king.

When we come to the kingdom of God, our hearts should mingle with His, with a whole heart.

> *Also it shall be, when he sits on the throne of his kingdom, that he shall write for himself a copy of this law in a book, from the one before the priests, the Levites. And it shall be with him, and he shall read it all the days of his life, that he may learn to fear the LORD his God and*

be careful to observe all the words of this law and these statutes, that his heart may not be lifted above his brethren, that he may not turn aside from the commandment to the right hand or to the left, and that he may prolong his days in his kingdom, he and his children in the midst of Israel.
                                          DEUT. 17:18–20

When the king obeys the words of the Lord, he will fulfill his destiny. When we have a whole heart to serve the Lord, He will also lead us into our destiny. Our destiny will be found when we remain in the sphere of God's kingdom. Because Jesus is living inside of us, He has given all the power and authority to kings. All the rulers in this world were appointed by God, and He has given His authority to them. So, to be a king, you need to be appointed by God. The book of Romans tells us that every ruler is appointed by God (Rom.13).

We need to understand the function of a king. The anointing itself signified the consecration to an office. The word *king,* in symbolic language, signifies "the possessor of supreme power," whether that power is lodged in one or more persons.

By me kings reign,
And rulers decree justice.
By me princes rule, and nobles,
All the judges of the earth
                    PROV. 8:15–16, EMPHASIS MINE

Kings are the ones who lead a kingdom. When the Holy Spirit came upon us, God's kingdom had already been established.

Jesus said, "But if I cast out demons by the Spirit of God, surely the kingdom of God has come upon you."
                    MATT. 12:28

Kings are God's servants and the only representatives of our Lord. As kings, we need to serve each other.

The Functions of a King

There are several functions that we fulfill while under the anointing of a king.

1) We are to reign and rule.

To *reign* means "to exercise sovereign power; to prevail and have widespread influence." To *rule* means "to exercise authority or to govern." An effective and great king must be a conqueror of many lands. In other words, he has to have possession of a great degree of territory.

> *God blessed them, and God said to them, "Be fruitful and multiply; fill the earth and subdue it; have dominion over the fish of the sea, over the birds of the air, and over every living thing that moves on the earth.*
> GEN. 1:28

God wanted mankind to multiply and have dominion over the earth.

This is the same privilege that God has given to us because of our identity in Christ and where we are seated. Kings are seated on the throne. We are seated in heavenly places, and we need to rule and reign in this world—and over our enemies. God has given us this authority and power over our enemies. But instead of our exercising this power, the enemy has infiltrated the church and weakened her, stealing what God has given. Now, God is restoring His power and authority back to the church after disarming the enemy at the cross.

> *[Christ] wiped out the handwriting of requirements that was against us, which was contrary to us. And He has taken it out of the way, having nailed it to the cross. Having disarmed principalities and powers, He made a public spectacle of them, triumphing over them in it.*
> COL. 2:14–15

This is the king's anointing that we have been given. We have the power to exercise our authority in Christ.

2) We are to create laws or rules.

In the Old Testament, kings proclaimed and taught the law, as well as judging wisely and righteously.

> *And all Israel heard of the judgment which the king had rendered; and they feared the king, for they saw that the wisdom of God was in him to administer justice.*
> 1 KINGS 3:28

In this way, we are to judge the world. The church has to make laws and rules that reflect the standards of God. This is where the church is currently weak. We don't know how to bring about judgment, instead we believe that the Lord will do this at the end. But the Almighty King has appointed us to bring this about.

The Anointing of a Prophet

Secondly, we have been given the anointing of a prophet. In the Old Testament, prophets were called **roeh**, which means "a seer." A seer is a person who sees things. The prophets in the Old Testament could "see" what would happen in the future. However, the tasks of the prophets were sometimes dangerous. One biblical example would be the prophet Micah. When he brought the message of truth to the king through a prophecy, the king tried to kill him. When we sometimes bring the truth to the people, they may criticize us or otherwise attack us. People don't always want to hear the truth. When we try to speak the truth to secular people, they don't always want to hear it.

The main role of the prophet was to bear God's words while teaching, reproving, correcting, and training in righteousness. The prophets were messengers of God.

When you have a prophetic anointing on your life, you will begin to see things that have already happened—and that will happen in the future. Many of the Old Testament characters were prophets. Noah was a prophet: He warned the people of the coming judgment of God on the earth. If he had not known about the coming judgment of God, he would not have invited the people into the ark to be saved. Because he invited people into the ark, he perceived what would take place in the future.

In the Greek, the word *prophet* means "interpreter." A prophet is someone who speaks forth, interpreting God's words for the people. The Hebrew word for *prophet* is *nabi.*, which means "to bubble forth like a fountain." When we speak a prophecy, it often comes out like a bubble. Unfortunately, many people believe that the act of prophesying is very difficult—this is not necessarily the case.

We need to understand what the prophets of the Bible actually did. But in order to understand what they did, we first need to understand their functions.

The Functions of a Prophet
1) The prophets were men of God.

The prophets were people who did not compromise with the world. Their passion and burning desire was to see God's Kingdom come about in the lives of the people and the nations. They were dedicated to this one purpose and cause. People would immediately recognize someone to be a man of God, or a prophet. An example of one such man of God was Samuel.

> *And he said to him, "Look now, there is in this city a **man of God**, and he is an honorable man; all that he says surely comes to pass. So let us go there; perhaps he can show us the way that we should go."*
> 1 SAM. 9:6, EMPHASIS MINE

This passage of scripture is describing what happened when the donkeys of Kish, Saul's father were lost. Saul and his servant had gone to find the donkeys, but they were unsuccessful. The servant asked that they go see Samuel; he knew that the man of God could tell them where the donkeys were. The servant recognized Samuel as a "man of God," a prophet.

2) The prophets were messengers of God.

The prophets were given specific messages from God to pass on to the people and the nations. Their mission was to deliver these important messages, regardless of what the outcome or the results may be. They were a lot like a pizza-delivery person today: They did not make the pizza (the message from God), but they delivered it to the people. That was their job. One example of a person who fulfilled this prophetic office would be Isaiah.

> Also I heard the voice of the Lord, saying:
> "Whom shall I send,
> And who will go for Us?"
> Then I said, "Here am I! Send me." And He said, "**Go,
> and tell** this people."
>
> ISA. 6:8–9, EMPHASIS MINE

God wondered whom He could send to give the people of Israel an important message. Isaiah offered himself for the mission, and God gave him the message to tell the people.

3) The prophets were to be watchmen.

The prophets were also called "watchmen." Watchmen were those people who had the job of watching out for coming danger. They were posted on top of ancient castles, and they kept up an intent watch to warn of coming trouble or attacks. Represented as warning voices, they watched through the night as others slept. To be a "warning voice" meant that you had to be alert at all times. Prophets were on the alert all the time, in order to hear from God and warn the people or nation.

> The word of the LORD came to me, saying, "Son of man, I have made you a **watchman** for the house of Israel; therefore hear a word from My mouth, and give them warning from Me."
>
> EZEK. 3:17, EMPHASIS MINE

God called Ezekiel to be a watchman for the house of Israel. He was to warn the people concerning the things he heard from God. Although the people would not listen to him, he still told them of the coming judgment and wrath of God.

For Today

When we have the prophetic anointing in our lives today, we, too, have the tasks of a prophet. We need to speak forth the Word of God. We need to be the voices that God uses to warn the people. We need to point the people in the right direction. Prophets always pointed the way for the people. They always heralded a message of repentance and of turning back to God. One way that we can share this message today is through the gift of prophecy. God wants us to prophesy and seek His gifts to edify the body of Christ.

> Pursue love, and desire spiritual gifts, but **especially that you may prophesy**. For he who speaks in a tongue does not speak to men but to God, for no one understands him;
> however, in the spirit he speaks mysteries. But he who prophesies speaks edification and exhortation and comfort to men.
> 1 COR. 14:1-3, EMPHASIS MINE

Paul was telling that we should desire spiritual gifts, and of all of the spiritual gifts, we should desire to prophesy. The Scriptures tell us to eagerly desire prophecy! We need the prophetic gifts now more than ever in our world.

Prophecy is used for three purposes:

> But he who prophesies speaks **edification** and **exhortation** and **comfort to men**.
> 1 COR. 14:3, EMPHASIS MINE

Prophecy is to be used to edify, exhort, and comfort the body of Christ, in order to build up the church.

Everyone Can Prophesy

Not only should we desire to receive prophecy, but we all should desire to prophesy. God has designed it so that everyone can prophesy. The gift of prophecy is not only for pastors and other leaders. It is given to all who desire it.

> *For you can **all prophesy** one by one, that all may learn*
> *and all may be encouraged.*
> 1 Cor. 14:31, emphasis mine

We are God's sheep, and His sheep always have the right to hear His voice.

> *Jesus said, "**My sheep hear My voice,** and I know them,*
> *and they follow Me."*
> John 10:27, emphasis mine

The gift of prophecy and the office of a prophet are two different things. Just because you can prophesy, this does not mean you are a prophet. We all have the spirit of prophecy, and everyone can prophesy. With this gift of prophecy, you can frequently be used in the prophetic. But the office of a prophet is one of the fivefold ministry gifts, and it is Jesus who chooses you as a prophet.

> *The word of the Lord came to me, saying:*
> *"Before I formed you in the womb I knew you;*
> *Before you were born I sanctified you;*
> *I ordained you a **prophet** to the nations."*
> Jer. 1:4–5, emphasis mine

The prophet Jeremiah was ordained, before he was born, to be a prophet to the nations. A person's fulfillment of this office of a prophet is something that God alone ordains.

Jesus was recognized as a prophet.

> *Then those men, when they had seen the sign that Jesus did, said, "This is truly the Prophet who is to come into the world."*
> JOHN 6:14

The prophets were the ones who spoke the Word of God. They reminded the people to turn their hearts back to God. They brought news of what God was doing in their time.

Today God has given us a prophet's anointing because He wants us to be His spokesmen in this world. He wants us to bring the Word of God to the people.

The Anointing of a Priest

God has also given us the priest's anointing, and called us to be priests before Him. God tells us that we are special people because we belong to Him.

> *You are a chosen generation, **a royal priesthood**, a holy nation, His own special people, that you may proclaim the praises of Him who called you out of darkness into His marvelous light; who once were not a people but are now the people of God, who had not obtained mercy but now have obtained mercy.*
> 1 PET. 2:9–10, EMPHASIS MINE

That's why we need to show, through our lives, the praises that God deserves. People need to see God praised through our worship to Him. Every single day of our life, we need to show forth our praises to God. We must also understand mercy and grace. Mercy always deals with the past, and grace deals with the present and the future.

God has promised us this through Moses:

> *"You have seen what I did to the Egyptians, and how I bore you on eagles' wings and brought you to Myself. Now therefore, if you will indeed obey My voice and keep My covenant, then you shall be a special treasure to Me above all people; for all the earth is Mine. And you shall be to Me a **kingdom of priests** and a holy nation."*
>
> EX. 19:4–6, EMPHASIS MINE

Through Moses, God is prophetically telling us that we, today, will be priests in His kingdom. But with this promise comes a condition; God said, "If you will hear and obey My voice, you will be a special treasure to Me, and you will be above all the people." God has told Moses that the earth belongs to Him. And because the earth belongs to God, we are therefore the owners of this earth. This proclamation limits the authority that Satan has over the earth. If we look back to Genesis 3:1, we can see that Satan was actually one of the beasts of the earth and more craftier than any other beasts of the field. If Satan was one of the beasts, then we know that he had limited authority. Satan came in the form of a serpent in the Old Testament and now in the New Testament, he takes the form of a dragon. He still has a mouth to speak forth lies and deception to people (Rev. 12:15-16, 1 John 4:1-6). However, he still has limited power over us. That's why God gave Adam the right to take dominion over the beasts of the earth. Why is that? God has given mankind all the power and authority to have dominion over the earth, including Satan. Satan has never had legal right in the earth.

In the Old Testament, the priests officiated worship by making various offerings on behalf of the nation and by leading the people to confess their sins. If you take another look at the Old Testament, you will see that the Levites were always assistants to the priests. The priests always took care of the tabernacle and the temple, in addition to performing other minor tasks, such as: providing music, serving as door keepers, and preparing the sacrifices and other offerings. Priests also acted as the mediators between man and God. They made all of the blood sacrifices (see Lev. 4:20–31). Without the shedding of blood, there is no remission of sins. Blood was shed because of our sins.

Without the blood, the priests' service was meaningless.

Today, we must always deal with situations and problems with the blood of Jesus Christ. Without His shed blood, we would not be able to enter into the Holy of Holies. God is calling us not to be mere ordinary priests, but high priests.

> *Therefore, holy brethren, partakers of the heavenly calling, consider the Apostle and **High Priest** of our confession, Christ Jesus.*
> HEB. 3:1, EMPHASIS MINE

The word for *high priest* in the Hebrew is *Ha-kohen*. God has made us high priests through Jesus Christ. We are "high priests" because we are not under the order of Levites but we are under the order of King Melchizedek. Because we have received the Holy Spirit, we have the authority and power to forgive someone's sin.

> *When [Jesus] had said this, He breathed on them, and said to them, "Receive the Holy Spirit. If you forgive the **sins of any**, **they are forgiven them**; if you retain the sins of any, they are retained."*
> JOHN 20:22–23, EMPHASIS MINE

Even when Jesus was dealing with sick people, He told them that their sins were forgiven. Jesus is the great High Priest who lives inside of us. He enables us to speak forgiveness to others. This should encourage us when we pray for other people, because if there is someone who is sick or possessed by a demon, we have the power and authority to forgive their sins in the name of Jesus. Also, as we pray for other nations, we can use this prayer as an intercession. We can pray on behalf of the nations, to ask for their forgiveness and to forgive their ancestral sins.

One of the tasks of a high priest is to deal with three types of sins. Once a year, before he entered into the Holy of Holies, the high priest first dealt with his own personal sins. Then he dealt with his family's and the other priests' sins. Finally, he dealt with the sins of the nation (Israel). So, by the time the priest finally entered the Holy of Holies and sprinkled the blood of the sacrifice on the mercy seat, his garment was spotted with blood. As soon as he left the Holy of Holies, the high priest took off his garment and hung it on one of the posts of the tabernacle; immediately, the blood stain on the garment was completely removed and became white as snow by the power of the Holy Spirit. The high priest would then stand before the Israelites and proclaim that their sins were forgiven. But without the clean garment, the high priest wouldn't have been able to proclaim forgiveness to the people.

High priests always deal with the nation; they do not deal with people on a one-by-one basis. We, as high priests, are responsible for the entire world.

The Responsibilities of a Priest

The priests had several different responsibilities.

1) They were mediators between the sinful people and a holy God (Num. 18:1).
2) They were messengers of the Lord (Mal. 2:7).
3) They were teachers of the Law to the people of Israel (Deut. 31:9–13; Lev. 10:10; Josh. 21).
4) They acted as judges, as if they were serving on the "supreme court" of Israel (Deut. 16:18–20; 17:8-13).

In special cases, the high priest would declare the will or judgment of God (Ex. 18:19–22; 28:30; Lev. 8:8; Deut. 33:8). The words *Urim* and *Thummim* mean "light" and "perfection." When the article *"the"* appears before these words in the Scriptures shows their distinctness. In Deuteronomy 33:8, an order was reversed by "thy Thummim and thy Urim." The word *Urim* appears alone in Numbers 27:21. In 1 Samuel 28:6, Saul was answered neither by dreams nor by Urim. The word *Thummim* is never cited by itself. When the high priest went in before the Lord, the Urim and Thummim were placed on his breastplate (Ex. 28:15–30; Lev. 8:8). These words were already familiar to Moses and the people at that particular time. When he was desiring counsel to guide Israel, Joshua was directed to "stand before Eleazar the priest, who should ask it for him after the judgment of Urim before Jehovah" (Num 27:21). Regarding Levi, from whom the whole priestly and levitical stock sprang, the Scriptures say, "Your Thummim and Your Urim be with Your Holy One" (Deut. 33:8-9). In Ezra 2:63, those who could not prove their priestly descent were excluded from the priesthood "till a priest could consult with the Urim and Thummim." God sometimes made His will known through the Urim and Thummim, and every time the high priest had to make a decision, he used the Urim and Thummim.

Special Note: The Anointing of the Old Testament Saints

We have learned that we have a threefold anointing in Christ. We have the anointing of a king, a prophet, and a priest. This anointing has been given for one purpose and that is to judge the world. Aside from the threefold anointing, being in Christ has an additional benefit. Consider for a moment the Old Testament saints: prophets like Isaiah, Jeremiah, Ezekiel, Amos, Micah, and Hosea, to name a few. Think of other saints, such as the prophets Samuel, Elijah, and Elisha; or the kings, such as Josiah, Hezekiah, and even David. Each of these men had a special anointing from God. But in fact, if we are in Christ, we also have all of the anointing of the Old Testament saints! What the Old Testament saints had was a partial anointing. They could not function in the fullness of the anointing because Christ was not in them. In Christ, all the anointing of the Old Testament saints is contained, and now that anointing is also in us.

Because Christ is God Himself, the full anointing is already in Him. And because we are in Christ, the full anointing is already in us. With that truth in hand, all of the Old Testament saints' anointing can be released and made available for us to use now, in this present day. Many Christians don't realize this wonderful truth: that God has given us everything in Christ. What Christ has is *all* of the anointing. We need to take a closer look at some of the Old Testament saints' anointing.

Let's start with the example of Daniel. Today, we have the anointing that Daniel had: the anointing to influence the government. The first time that Daniel interpreted a dream, he was promoted to be a ruler, and he eventually became the chief administrator of all the wise men in Babylon. We have the same anointing—to reveal the plans of God to other people. God gives us the anointing to understand dreams and mysteries in order to unveil the purpose of His will.

> *Then the king **promoted Daniel** and gave him many great gifts; and he made him ruler over the whole province of Babylon, and **chief administrator over all the wise men** of Babylon.*
> DAN. 2:48, EMPHASIS MINE

The second time Daniel interpreted a dream, the king declared that God was the true God, and he began to praise the God of Daniel.

> *"At the end of the time I, Nebuchadnezzar, lifted my eyes to heaven, and my understanding returned to me; and I blessed the Most High and praised and honored Him who lives forever:*
> *For His dominion is an everlasting dominion,*
> *And His kingdom is from generation to generation."*
> DAN. 4:34, EMPHASIS MINE

Daniel influenced the government of his day with his spiritual interpretation of dreams. This anointing, to influence the governments of our world, is in us, too. We have the anointing to bring our government to the understanding that God is the true God, that He is the Most High, and that He is to be praised forever and evermore. Hallelujah!

Another example of an Old Testament anointing that we still have today is the anointing that was on Esther. Esther did, in fact, influence the king, or government, of her day, but her anointing was for the purpose of saving the Jewish race. Her anointing salvaged many lives that otherwise would have been murdered. Her anointing reversed the decree of death over her people.

> *Instead, Haman sought to destroy all the Jews who were throughout the whole kingdom of Ahasuerus.*
> ESTHER 3:6

> *By these letters the king permitted the Jews who were in every city to gather together and protect their lives—to destroy, kill, and annihilate all the forces of any people or province that would assault them, both little children and women, and to plunder their possessions.... And in every province and city, wherever the king's command and decree came, the Jews had joy and gladness, a feast and a holiday.*
> ESTHER 8:11, 17

> *On the day that the enemies of the Jews had hoped to overpower them, the opposite occurred, in that the Jews themselves overpowered those who hated them.*
> ESTHER 9:1

We have the anointing to save lives in this world. We can make intercession for other nations, praying that God would save that land and the people in it. Teams need to be raised up to go into new territories and stand in the gap, interceding on behalf of those nations of the world.

Let's take a look at the anointing that was on Nehemiah's life. His anointing was that of a reformer. When he heard that the walls of Jerusalem were destroyed, he was dismayed, and so he asked the king for permission to go and rebuild the walls of Jerusalem. As he did so, certain people began to criticize his work, and they became a hindrance or a stumbling block to him. But Nehemiah completed the work, and in the end, the walls were constructed more solidly than they had been in their original state, before they had been destroyed. Nehemiah's anointing was that of reviving and reforming, not only the walls, but also the people of God. He helped rebuild the shattered walls in peoples' lives by rebuilding the walls of Jerusalem and bringing hope to the people. This same anointing is on our lives today. We have the same anointing—to help restore the broken walls in peoples' lives and to restore hope in their hearts.

God has given us the threefold anointing for one purpose: so that we would be judges in this world. Because we are in Christ, we should expect to function in the full anointing. God has placed this full anointing in us in order to empower us to deliver people out of the bondage of darkness. We need to go forth in this anointing and take action.

CHAPTER EIGHT

The Anointing to Judge

Called to Judge

Throughout the Scriptures, God raised up judges because His people were oppressed. The Hebrew word for *judge* is *shaphat*, which means "deliverer." In the Old Testament, God sent judges to help the people who were oppressed, but they did not listen to them. Instead, they played the harlot, which meant that they began to worship other idols.

> *Nevertheless, the LORD* **raised up judges** *who delivered them out of the hand of those who plundered them.* **Yet they would not listen to their judges,** *but they played the harlot with other gods, and bowed down to them. They turned quickly from the way in which their fathers walked, in obeying the commandments of the LORD; they did not do so.*
> JUDG. 2:16–17, EMPHASIS MINE

The people did not obey what had God commanded them. They refused to listen to His judges, and this opened the way for them to worship other gods.

The purpose of the threefold anointing is to raise up judges and to deliver people from their oppression and bondages.

> *And when the LORD raised up judges for them, the LORD was with the judge and delivered them out of the hand of their enemies all the days of the judge; for the LORD was moved to pity by their groaning because of those who oppressed them and harassed them."*
> JUDG. 2:18, EMPHASIS MINE

We are now in this world, saved due to the grace of God. God has given us the anointing to judge in our world. This anointing to judge means that we are to be deliverers of those who are oppressed, people who have been held in bondage and afflicted by the enemy in this world. People who don't know the Lord are being attacked by the enemy, but God is raising us up to act and be judges of this world.

If you look at the court system in our world, what is the role of the judge? The judge pronounces the sentence, or punishment. The judge is to proclaim if someone is guilty or innocent. When the judge strikes the gavel, he sentences the guilty.

God has called us to be judges, to act with the authority of a judge. This allows us the power to give the enemy a sentence, or a punishment. We have the authority to sentence Satan to whatever fate he deserves. Christians should be sentencing the enemy, but instead, they are being constantly beaten up by him

> *Having **disarmed principalities and powers**, [Christ] made a public spectacle of them, **triumphing over them** in it.*
> COL. 2:15, EMPHASIS MINE

This verse tells us that Jesus has already triumphed over the enemy through the cross. By His death on the cross, He sentenced the enemy and disarmed his power. Because Satan has been disarmed, he has no weapons to use against us.

> *No weapon formed against you shall prosper.*
> Isa. 54:17

Many Christians do not believe this truth, but they need to know that all the power and authority have been given to us. Because we have this power and authority, we are called to be rulers of this world. We are called to judge the nations—not by the world's court systems, but by the court system of heavenly authority that has been given to us by God. We need to believe that we are powerful people because Jesus paid the price on the cross. Through the cross, God has given us all the power of heaven and earth. He promised us that everything is under our feet.

> *Thus says the LORD,*
> *"Heaven is My throne,*
> *And earth is My footstool."*
> Isa. 66:1

What is the purpose of a footstool? It is to allow a person to sit down and rest. True resting will only take place in the Spirit of God. If we would only rest in the Spirit of God, we would not fear or worry about anything. True Sabbath rest does not occur only on a Saturday or a Sunday; resting in the Spirit of God can occur any day of the week! Because God has put everything under our feet, we can rest in the Spirit.

> *He will subdue the peoples under us,*
> *And the nations under our feet.*
> Ps. 47:3

What nations are under our feet? All the nations that are Satan's are under our feet. Everything is under the church.

> [His mighty power] He worked in Christ when He raised Him from the dead and seated Him at His right hand in the heavenly places, far above all principality and power and might and dominion, and every name that is named, not only in this age but also in that which is to come. And He put all things under His feet, and gave Him to be head over all things to the church, which is His body, the fullness of Him who fills all in all.
> EPH. 1:20–23

Because everything is under the church, the enemy does not have any power.

> Jesus said, "And I also say to you that you are Peter, and on this rock I will build My church, and the **gates of Hades shall not prevail against it**. And I will give you the keys of the kingdom of heaven, and whatever you bind on earth will be bound in heaven, and whatever you loose on earth will be loosed in heaven."
> MATT. 16:18–19, EMPHASIS MINE

Because God has put everything under our feet, we need to be rulers over everything. We need to understand the true meaning of judging the world.

> Jesus said, "Behold, I give you the **authority** to trample on serpents and scorpions, and over all the **power** of the enemy, and nothing shall by any means hurt you."
> LUKE 10:19, EMPHASIS MINE

Here is the underlying principle of this verse: The serpent is the snake. Where does its poison come from? The poison is on his teeth. When you step on the serpent's head, the enemy will not be able to poison anyone again. When we smash his head, he will not be able to do anything. We need to step on his head more often.

Why does Jesus use this particular parable to teach us? All poison comes from the serpent's head, where its teeth are. If you let snakes move, they can attack you, but if you step on their heads, they are not able to move. God has placed the enemy under our feet. Sometimes we don't realize that we are actually stepping on a snake's head, but this is the time when we need to smash and crush his head. One way to do this is to always dance before the Lord. When we dance before the Lord, we are actually stomping and trampling on the enemy's head. Hallelujah!

*God stands in the **congregation of the mighty**;*
He judges among the gods.
How long will you judge unjustly,
And show partiality to the wicked?
Defend the poor and fatherless;
Do justice to the afflicted and needy.
Deliver the poor and needy;
Free them from the hand of the wicked.
They do not know, nor do they understand;
They walk about in darkness;
All the foundations of the earth are unstable.
I said, "You are gods,
And all of you are children of the Most High.
But you shall die like men,
And fall like one of the princes."
Arise, O God, judge the earth;
For You shall inherit all nations.

Ps. 82

Let me break down this psalm for you. Who is the congregation of the mighty? We are the mighty congregation. We are also called to judge the people justly. The foundation of the earth is unstable. Because the foundations are unstable, we need to make them stable. Jesus is the stable foundation. Hallelujah!

How many people are out there who believe that God has already judged this earth? God gave the right to judge to His Son. Now, the Son has given that right to judge to us.

> *Proclaim this among the nations:*
> *"Prepare for war!*
> *Wake up the mighty men,*
> *Let all the men of war draw near,*
> *Let them come up.*
> *Beat your plowshares into swords*
> *And your pruning hooks into spears;*
> *Let the weak say, 'I am strong.'"*
> *Assemble and come, all you nations,*
> *And gather together all around.*
> *Cause Your mighty ones to go down there, O LORD.*
> *"Let the nations be wakened, and come up to the Valley*
> *of Jehoshaphat;*
> *For there I will sit to judge all the surrounding nations.*
> *Put in the sickle, for the harvest is ripe.*
> *Come, go down;*
> *For the winepress is full,*
> *The vats overflow—*
> *For their wickedness is great."*
> *Multitudes, multitudes in the valley of decision!*
> *For the day of the LORD is near in the valley of decision.*
> JOEL 3:9–14

Warfare

God wants us to prepare for war. The instrument used for harvest and the weapon used for battle is the same. What does this mean? How can we use the same instrument for harvest as a weapon of warfare? God is commanding us to change our harvest instruments into weapons of warfare, but this requires the anointing of God. With the anointing, we can change these two back and forth, from an instrument of harvest to a weapon; and from a weapon back to an instrument of harvest.

We also need to "come up to the valley of Jehoshaphat." Where is the valley of Jehoshaphat? It is the place of "decision making." When we go to this valley, we go there to make a decision. We need to make up our minds—by the power of the Holy Spirit.

> *Then I looked, and behold, a white cloud, and on the cloud sat one like the Son of Man, having on His head a golden crown, and in His hand a sharp sickle. And another angel came out of the temple, crying with a loud voice to Him who sat on the cloud, "Thrust in Your sickle and reap, for the time has come for You to reap, for the harvest of the earth is ripe." So He who sat on the cloud thrust in His sickle on the earth, and the earth was reaped.*
> Rev. 14:14–16, EMPHASIS MINE

Where is this sickle? When we go into the harvest field, we must use the sickle to bring in the crops. So, the sickle is in our hands. On whose hand was the sharp sickle placed? It was on Jesus' hand. And who is "His hand?" We are His hands! So, we are the sharp sickle. The world will be reaped through us because we are His hand. That's why God trusts His sickle. God has made us to be the tools for the harvest. We need each other to evangelize the world.

The Result of Standing As a Judge

When we begin to judge by God's authority, people will start coming to us. When we stand as judges of this world, people will begin to climb up to where we are. That is why we need to live by the Spirit of God and under the power of the Holy Spirit.

> *Now it shall come to pass in the latter days*
> *That the mountain of the LORD's house*
> *Shall be established on the top of the mountains,*

And shall be exalted above the hills;
And peoples shall flow to it.
Many nations shall come and say,
"Come, and let us go up to the mountain of the LORD,
To the house of the God of Jacob;
He will teach us His ways,
And we shall walk in His paths."
For out of Zion the law shall go forth,
And the word of the LORD from Jerusalem.
He shall judge between many peoples,
And rebuke strong nations afar off;
They shall beat their swords into plowshares;
And their spears into pruning hooks;
Nation shall not lift up sword against nation,
Neither shall they learn war anymore.
                    MICAH 4:1–3, EMPHASIS MINE

What wonderful verses! We won't need to come down to the people because they will already see that we are the true light of this world. From this passage, we learn several things. First, we are on top of the mountain, and people will begin to come to us. If this is not happening in our lives, then we have a problem. Second, people need to expect us to teach them the ways of God. Third, they should also expect us to walk in His path, the path of Jesus Christ. Fourth, the law will go out from Zion. Zion represents the church, and so this means that the law should go out from the church. We should be the law of this earth; the law of God and the Word of God should come forth from us. This is why Christians need to arise and stand by the power of the Holy Spirit. We need to be rulers of this world. We need to change the world by the power of God for Jesus Christ.

 When you see this, your heart shall rejoice,
And your bones shall flourish like grass;
The hand of the LORD shall be known to His servants,
And His indignation to His enemies.
For behold, the LORD will come with fire
And with His chariots, like a whirlwind,

To render His anger with fury,
And His rebuke with flames of fire.
For by fire and by His sword
The LORD will judge all flesh;
And the slain of the LORD shall be many.
ISA. 66:14–16, EMPHASIS MINE

How Do We Judge the World?

We are to judge the world by fire and by His sword—and then the Lord will judge all flesh. So, we judge this world with **the Word of God** and with **the power of the Holy Spirit.** These two things can't be separated; one can't work without the other. We need to be seated properly in order to judge this world. If we do not sit with Christ on the throne, we will have no power to judge.

Jesus appointed the Kingdom to us, just as God appointed it to Jesus.

*Jesus said, "But you are those who have continued with Me in My trials. And I bestow upon you a kingdom, just as My Father bestowed one upon Me, **that you may eat and drink at My table in My kingdom, and sit on thrones judging the twelve tribes of Israel.**"*
LUKE 22:28–30, EMPHASIS MINE

The Kingdom of God

Because we are true disciples of Jesus Christ, He has appointed His kingdom unto us, so that we can eat and drink with Him in His kingdom, judging the twelve tribes of Israel. God is the One who prepares our food for us, because we are at His table in His Kingdom. Many preachers try to prepare food for their flocks through other means, such as Bible commentaries and other references. These tools should never take the place of hearing from God directly! Every preacher, leader, or minister who is involved in teaching the Bible needs to remember that Jesus Himself will prepare our food for us.

We will also sit with Him, judging the twelve tribes of Israel. God wants to judge the entire world through our lives. If the Kingdom of God is established in our hearts by the power of the Holy Spirit, then we are seated with Him on the throne of God. If this is the case, every time we hear His voice, we will be judging the people and nations. That's why when the Holy Spirit comes upon us, we will receive power, and we will be witnesses to Judea, to Jerusalem, to Samaria, and to the entire world (Matt. 19:28, Luke 22:30).

When you receive the Holy Spirit, you become a martyr for the Lord. Martyrs, or witnesses, lay down their lives for the Lord. So, when the Holy Spirit comes upon us and explodes inside of our hearts, then we will destroy the kingdom of Satan and establish the Kingdom of God. God establishes His kingdom inside of us in order to pour down His Spirit upon us, with grace and truth, so that we can manifest the nature of God in our lives.

The Condition of Being Judges

> *"Thus says the LORD of hosts:*
> *'If you will walk in **My ways,***
> *And if you will keep **My command,***
> *Then you shall also **judge My house,***
> *And likewise have charge of **My courts**;*
> *I will give you places to walk*
> *Among these who stand here.'"*
> ZECH. 3:7, EMPHASIS MINE

In this verse, God gave us a condition, as we become judges. The condition was to walk in His ways and keep His commands. We can only judge by hearing His voice. We can only judge those whom He commands us to judge. We are His saints who judge the world.

> *Let the saints be joyful in glory;*
> *Let them sing aloud on their beds.*

Let the high praises of God be in their mouth,
*And **a two-edged sword in their hand,***
To execute vengeance on the nations,
And punishments on the peoples;
To bind their kings with chains,
And their nobles with fetters of iron;
*To **execute** on them the written judgment—*
*This honor **have all His saints**.*
Praise the LORD.
PS. 149:5–9, EMPHASIS MINE

We have been given a two-edged sword with which to cut off all the work of the enemy and execute judgment on the enemy and wickedness.

CHAPTER NINE

The Restoration of the Anointing

A New Creation

When you are in Christ, you become a new creation. We need to understand the importance of this truth in our lives.

> *Therefore, if anyone is **in Christ, he is a new creation;** old things have passed away; behold, all things have become new.*
> 2 COR. 5:17, EMPHASIS MINE

Reconciliation between God and man takes place through Jesus Christ. We are the children of God. Second Corinthians 5:17 does not say, "if anyone is in Jesus," but it says, "if anyone is *in Christ.*" The word *Christ* means "Messiah; the Anointed one." If we are in Christ, we are the anointed ones. But if we're not under the anointing of the Holy Spirit, we're not new creations. Without the anointing of God, we can't become new creations. Many people say that they're in Christ, but they still hold on to "old" things. Many of us still hold onto our traditions and cultures. Being a new creation means that our spirit, soul, and flesh are made completely new. Without becoming new creations, we will never reach to the full stature of Christ. We will never reach the high level of potential we could reach in God.

Citizens of the Kingdom

The primary question we need to ask ourselves is, "Why can't we change, or transform?" The answer is that our minds keep thinking, *I am who I am.* This is the problem that prevents us from growing up and transforming in Christ. The Bible says that old things have passed away, but we forget that we are dealing with Kingdom culture, and not our own culture. That is what it means to be in the new creation. It doesn't matter what nationality we are—we are citizens of heaven. But if we continue to hold on to our old mentality, that we are a specific nationality, we will never grow up, and we will never be transformed in Christ. We need to break out of our old mentality, for we no longer belong to any nationality here on earth. We no longer need to keep our own culture in life, because we are now living in the Kingdom of heaven. This mentality can only be broken by the anointing of God. We must replace our old mentality with the Word of God. Yesterday has passed away.

The apostle Paul declared that he was crucified daily. What did he mean by that? He meant that every day he needed to re-new himself before the Lord. He had to remind himself of who he was in Christ. He needed to forget his old lifestyle, in order to walk in the new. If we keep worrying about things that have passed, we will never be able to walk in maturity in the future.

Don't Think about the Past

> *Thus says the* LORD,
> **"Do not remember the former things,**
> **Nor consider the things of old.**
> *Behold,* **I will do a new thing,**
> *Now it shall spring forth;*

Shall you not know it?
I will even make a road in the wilderness
And rivers in the desert."

ISA. 43:18–19, EMPHASIS MINE

God commands us not to remember the old things—not to ponder them. As we commit to obey this command, God will begin to do new things in our life. If we continue to keep thinking about the old things in our life, God can't do new things in our lives, and we won't be able to change. We should not think about the old things that have passed away. Every Christian needs to focus on the present and the future. Yesterday will never come back to us. God wants us to focus on the present and future.

Restoration of All

God may send Jesus Christ...whom heaven must receive
*until the **times of restoration of all things,** which God*
has spoken by the mouth of all His holy prophets since
the world began.

ACTS 3:20–21, EMPHASIS MINE

God will be receiving Jesus Christ in heaven until all things are restored. Restoration must take place before Jesus Christ comes back. God appointed His Kingdom to us. The Kingdom of God depends upon us because the Holy Spirit is already inside of us. For this reason, our lives are very important. Wherever we go, the Kingdom of God goes with us. Until we have the full anointing and do whatever He asks us to do, Jesus can't come back. Take a look at the Christians in this world. Are they truly ready for their Groom to come back? Not at all! No groom would want to marry an immature bride. But unfortunately, ministers are still changing the diapers of the spiritual infants in the church. Until Christians become mature, Jesus can't return.

Breakthrough Anointing

> *It shall come to pass **in that day***
> *That his burden will be taken away from your shoulder,*
> *And his yoke from your neck,*
> *And the yoke will be destroyed because of the anointing*
> *oil.*
> ISA. 10:27, EMPHASIS MINE

The phrase *in that day* refers to the Day of Pentecost. When the Holy Spirit comes upon you, you will receive the anointing, and because of the anointing, your burden and yoke will be destroyed. Without the anointing of God, we can't break out of our sinful nature and all of our guilty feelings. The anointing destroys and removes everything sinful and impure from our lives. The anointing destroys all yokes and bondage. What do the words *burden* and *yoke* mean? The word *burden* signifies the sin nature. Sin is our burden. The word *yoke* signifies the slave mentality. The enemy has been controlling us like slaves. The enemy tries to control our lives by placing a chain around our necks and dragging us with him.

> ***Shake yourself from the dust**, arise;*
> *Sit down, O Jerusalem!*
> ***Loose yourself from the bonds of your neck,***
> *O captive daughter of Zion!*
> ISA. 52:2, EMPHASIS MINE

We were living in bondage, with chains around our necks, but now we are no longer slaves. When the anointing manifests itself in our lives, our burdens will be lifted, and our yokes will be taken from our necks. Hallelujah! We are no longer slaves and no longer sinners. We are the righteous ones who live by faith. Jesus Christ is our righteousness, and if we are "in Him," we are righteous, too. We are no longer sinners, but righteous people. Even though we may still sin, we can come before Him and ask for forgiveness, and He will forgive and wash all of our sins away. (1John1:9)

The Anointing Teaches All Things

> *But you have an **anointing from the Holy One,** and **you know all things.***
>
> 1 JOHN 2:20, EMPHASIS MINE

Because we have the anointing from the Holy One, we should know all things. But the sad thing is, we *don't* know all things. This occurs because we don't have the full anointing; if we had the full anointing, we would know everything.

> But the anointing which you have received from Him abides in you, and you do not need that anyone teach you; but as the same anointing teaches you concerning all things, and is true, and is not a lie, and just as it has taught you, you will abide in Him.
>
> 1 JOHN 2:27

So, how can we abide with Jesus Christ? We do this through the anointing of God. The anointing teaches us what Jesus taught His disciples. The anointing also helps us to discern things. If we are flowing in the anointing of God, we can discern spirits. Under the anointing of God, we will abide with Jesus, and He will abide with us. We must remember this:

The Heavenly Father is the **Anointer.**
Jesus Christ is the **Anointed One.**
The **Holy Spirit** provides the **anointing.**

If we are baptized in the Spirit, we are the anointed ones. So, the anointing teaches all; it discerns things in our lives, and the anointing will abide with us, and we will also abide with it. Since we are in Christ, we are living in the Garden of Eden.

> *For the LORD will comfort Zion;*
> *He will comfort all her waste places;*

He will make her wilderness like Eden,
And her desert like the garden of the LORD;
Joy and gladness will be found in it,
Thanksgiving and the voice of melody.

ISA. 51:3

Why God Has Anointed Us

There are two words used for the anointing: *charisma* and *chario*. *Chario* is used more with regard to religious service. *Charisma* is translated as the "anointing" or "unction."

The Spirit of the LORD *God is upon Me,*
Because the LORD *has anointed Me*
To **preach good tidings** *to the poor;*
He has sent Me **to heal the brokenhearted,**
To proclaim liberty *to the captives,*
And the opening of the prison to those who are bound;
To proclaim the acceptable year of the LORD,
And the day of vengeance of our God;
To comfort all who mourn;
To console those who mourn in Zion,
To give them beauty for ashes,
The oil of joy for mourning,
The garment of praise for the spirit of heaviness;
That they may be called trees of righteousness,
The planting of the LORD, *that He may be glorified.*

ISA. 61:1–3, EMPHASIS MINE

Jesus quoted this Scripture to let everyone know that they could be set free from all of their debts and bondages. It is the year of Jubilee for the people.

To understand why God has anointed us we need to look at the purpose of Christ's anointing. First, He was anointed to preach the Gospel; second, to heal the brokenhearted; third, to preach deliverance to the captives; fourth, to recover sight to the blind; fifth, to proclaim liberty to the captives; and finally, to preach the year of Jubilee. This is the purpose for which God anointed Jesus Christ.

Now, why is God anointing us today? Why did He give us power and authority? Why is He giving us wisdom? He is anointing us because He wants us to do the same things that Jesus did on the earth.

> *Jesus said, "Most assuredly, I say to you, he who believes in Me, **the works that I do he will do also; and greater works than these he will do** because I go to My Father."*
> JOHN 14:12, EMPHASIS MINE

We need this anointing, and we need to increase in it, too. When our anointing increases, we will have more freedom and liberty. And this is how we will go from glory to glory.

CHAPTER TEN

Releasing the Anointing in Your Life

How can we release the anointing in our own lives? How does it work? For the answers, we must look at the book of Genesis very carefully. Genesis 2 tells us about four rivers that flowed through the Garden of Eden. These rivers hold the key to how we can release the anointing in our lives.

Living Water of Joy

When we have the joy of the Lord, the living water inside of us will flow. God wants us to protect our joy in life from the things in this world that would try to take our joy away. Because we are not naturally Kingdom-oriented and we tend to focus on the flesh, we can easily miss out on walking in our calling. However, as we live out our calling, we know what we need to do. This is what gives us joy in our hearts. We need to have an abundance of joy flowing out of our lives. There are four stages that will occur when the river of joy flows out of our lives.

> *Now a river went out of Eden to water the garden, and from there it parted and became four riverheads. The name of the first is **Pishon**; it is the one which skirts the whole land of Havilah, where there is gold. And the gold of that land is good. Bdellium and the onyx stone are there.*
>
> GEN. 2:10–12, EMPHASIS MINE

In this verse, the phrase, "the river divided and became four rivers," can help to open up your spiritual eyes and understanding with regard to the anointing.

Four Stages of the Anointing

The first stage of releasing joy is to grow up. The word *pishon* in the Hebrew language means to "grow up." The words *land of Havilah* mean "hope," or "land of hope." They also mean "to bring forth." The word *gold* means "divine nature." When the river flows, you will first "grow up." This growing up means to grow up . When you grow up, the Promised Land will be a hope for you. Then, after you grow up and receive hope, you will be given a divine nature. This divine nature builds up our faith.

All of this means that we need to grow up, or mature, in our Christian walk. If we want to possess the Promised Land, we need to have the divine nature present in our lives. This divine nature is the nature of God. Our lives must be filled with the glory of God in order to drive out the enemies in our Promised Land and experience the full anointing in our lives. The divine nature builds up our faith because it separates us from the world. The word *bdellium* means "separation." We need to bring forth our divine nature by being separated from the world.

> *The name of the second river is **Gihon**; it is the one which goes around the whole land of Cush.*
>
> GEN. 2:13, EMPHASIS MINE

The second river is *Gihon*. The word *gihon* in the Hebrew language means to "break forth." After you grow up, you break forth. God wants to "break forth" all of the bondages out of our lives. We can't have true joy until we have been set free from all bondage. God wants to break things in our lives that cause hindrances or distractions. Once we are free from these things, we will have good reason to be joyful. This joy will enable us to overcome any obstacles we may face in life. We need to have this breakthrough in our lives so that we can be free to totally live for the cause of Christ. That's why the Bible tells us to crucify our flesh and our desires.

> *And those who are Christ's have crucified the flesh with its passions and desires.*
> GAL. 5:24

If you want a breakthrough in your life, you must first break out of the worldly things that are attached to you. Having things of the world attached to us will slow the process of a breakthrough in our life. All in all, this means that we should not compromise. We need to make a committed decision to follow Christ.

> *The name of the third river is **Hiddekel**; it is the one which goes toward the east of **Assyria**.*
> GEN. 2:14, EMPHASIS MINE

This river flows toward Assyria. The word *Assyria* means "blessing." The word *hiddekel* means "rapidly." So, this river will lead you to your blessing, and the joy that you experience will lead to your blessing even more rapidly. We will receive the blessings of God rapidly, once we break forth from our old life. We are missing some blessings in our life because we are not overflowing with joy. Rather, we consume our minds with the world, as we wonder how we can receive these blessings. We start to compare our things in the world with God's blessings. We assume that God wants to bless us in a material way, such as through a promotion, a raise, or a new car, just to name a few examples.

These are not the blessings the Bible is talking about. Our true blessing will come when our lives are filled with joy, joy that causes us to acknowledge and confess that He is all we need in life. Having Jesus should bring us all the contentment that we need in this life.

> *The fourth river is the **Euphrates**.*
> GEN. 2:14, EMPHASIS MINE

The last stage, or river, is the Euphrates. The word *Euphrates* means "fruitful" and "increase." The river flowing out of you will bring you to a place of increase in your life. God wants you to be fruitful. God is ready to give you the increase, but in order for that to happen, you first need to decrease. This is what John the Baptist confessed. He knew that he needed to decrease (see John 3:30).

We need to decrease our own agendas, so that God can increase His agenda in our lives. What has God been increasing in your life? Are you experiencing increase and fruitfulness? Do you know that this is your time to receive the increase? God wants to increase us, but we first need to decrease those things in our lives that prevent us from receiving this increase. What are the things in your life that distract you or pull you farther away from God? Are you ready to decrease those things in your life? If you are, then God has a special promise for you.

I want to mention that the tree of the knowledge of good and evil will be no more. There will be a new Paradise, and out of it will flow the river of the water of life.

> *And he showed me a pure **river of water of life**, clear as crystal, proceeding from the throne of God and of the Lamb. In the middle of its street, and on either side of the river, was the tree of life, which bore twelve fruits, each tree yielding its fruit every month. The leaves of the tree were for the healing of the nations. And there shall be no more curse, but the throne of God and of the Lamb shall*

be in it, and His servants shall serve Him. They shall see His face, and His name shall be on their foreheads. There shall be no night there: They need no lamp nor light of the sun, for the Lord God gives them light. And they shall reign forever and ever.

REV. 22:1–5, EMPHASIS MINE

You will show me the path of life;
In Your presence is fullness of joy;
At Your right hand are pleasures forevermore.

PS. 16:11, EMPHASIS MINE

There will only be joy in His presence.

The Process of the Anointing

We are the temple of the Holy Spirit.

Do you not know that you are the temple of God and that the Spirit of God dwells in you? If anyone defiles the temple of God, God will destroy him. For the temple of God is holy, which temple you are.

1 COR. 3:16–17, EMPHASIS MINE

Out of us should come forth the river of life. This flows from Jerusalem.

And in that day it shall be
That **living waters shall flow from Jerusalem,**
Half of them toward the eastern sea
And half of them toward the western sea;
In both summer and winter it shall occur.
And the LORD *shall be King over all the earth.*
In that day it shall be—
"The LORD *is one,"*
And His name one.

ZECH. 14:8–9, EMPHASIS MINE

The Hebrew word *jeru* means "righteousness," and the word *salem* means "peace." So, righteousness and peace will be flowing out of our lives.

Where is the throne of God and of the Lamb? It is actually in our hearts.

> *On the last day, that great day of the feast, Jesus stood and cried out, saying, "If anyone thirsts, let him come to Me and drink. He who believes in Me, as the Scripture has said, out of his heart will flow rivers of living water." But this He spoke concerning the Spirit, whom those believing in Him would receive; for the Holy Spirit was not yet given, because Jesus was not yet glorified.*
> JOHN 7:37–39

Healing water will come upon our lives when the anointing flows. This healing water comes down from the throne of God. We just found out that the throne of God is in our hearts. So, how do we release this out of our hearts? How can we release this healing water in our lives? In the book of Ezekiel, this is referred to as the river of the sanctuary. It is preceded in four steps.

> *Then he brought me back to the door of the temple; and there was water, flowing from under the threshold of the temple toward the east.*
> EZEK. 47:1

The process of the anointing starts from the temple. When the water comes down from the temple, that water becomes a river. When the river touches the sea, everything becomes alive, and everything is healed. The river works its way down, but the filling starts from the bottom and works its way up. Starting from your *ankles* to your *knees* to your *loins* and your *waist*, it continues to go up until you *sink* under the anointing.

> And when the man went out to the east with the line in his hand, he measured one thousand cubits, and he brought me through the waters; the **water came up to my ankles**.
>
> EZEK. 47:3, EMPHASIS MINE

The first step takes place when the water rises to your ankles. This occurs when you accept the Lord and get baptized by the Spirit. However, you may still want to do whatever you want, but God holds your ankles so that you don't run away and become separated from Him.

> *Again he measured one thousand and brought me through the waters; the **water came up to my knees**. Again he measured one thousand and brought me through; the **waters came up to my waist**.*
>
> EZEK. 47:4, EMPHASIS MINE

The second step occurs when the water rises to your knees. This is the time to know how to pray. This is the process of coming into the fullness of Christ.

The third step takes place when the water rises to your waist. When it is at your waist, it is hard to walk through the water.

Having some experience as a scuba diver, I know about water. When the water comes up to your waist, you can't move well, but you can still bend. The reason you can't move well in the water is because the water is exerting pressure and resistance against you.

All of the power in the human body comes out from the waist. If you have a disc problem, you won't be able to lift heavy things. This is the reason God holds your waist.

> *Again he measured one thousand, and it was a river that I could not cross; for the water was too deep, **water in which one must swim**, a river that could not be crossed.*
>
> EZEK. 47:5, EMPHASIS MINE

The last step takes place when we are completely submerged under the water. Once we are under the anointing, then we will begin to swim in the anointing, and we will see many miracles. This passage of scripture is not talking about natural water; it is talking about being completely covered by the Word of God and the Holy Spirit. So, we need to swim inside the Word of God in the Holy Spirit; this will then lead us to have a fruitful life.

Let's take a look at what is happening from the swimmer's point of view. If you see a wave coming and you try to swim against it, you will fail. However, if you go under it, you will pass. If you try to go against the world without being submerged in the Word of God, you will die spiritually. But if you go under the water, or under the anointing, you will pass and live through the world.

> *He said to me, "Son of man, have you seen this?" Then he brought me and returned me to the bank of the river. When I returned, there, along the bank of the river, were very many trees on one side and the other.*
> EZEK. 47:6–7

Is the Bible talking here about natural trees? When Jesus prayed for the blind man, the first thing that the blind man saw were some "trees walking." When the Bible talks about trees, it is referring to mankind.

Releasing the Anointing

God created mankind to give them joy in their hearts. God wants you to have this joy in your life. We are called to live a joyful life, regardless of the circumstances in which we find ourselves, because He created us to have joy. Joy was given to protect our lives. So how do we release joy in our lives? Paul clearly tells us the answer in 1 Thessalonians 5:

> **Rejoice always, pray without ceasing, in everything give thanks; for this is the will of God in Christ Jesus for you.**
> 1 THESS. 5:16–18, EMPHASIS MINE

And he does so again in Philippians 4:4

> **Rejoice in the Lord always,** *again I will say* **rejoice.**
> PHIL. 4:4, EMPHASIS MINE

Here are two other verses that demonstrate how we can release the anointing:

> *When the LORD brought back the captivity of Zion,*
> *We were like those who dream.*
> *Then **our mouth was filled with laughter,***
> *And **our tongue with singing.***
> *Then they said among the nations,*
> *"The LORD **has done great things for them."***
> *The LORD has done great things for us,*
> ***And we are glad.***
> *Bring back our captivity, O LORD,*
> *As the streams in the South.*
> *Those who sow in tears*
> ***Shall reap in joy.***
> *He who continually goes forth weeping,*
> *Bearing seed for sowing,*
> ***Shall doubtless come again with rejoicing,***
> *Bringing his sheaves with him.*
> PS. 126:1–6, EMPHASIS MINE

And one more time, I want to mention this verse:

> **"Do not sorrow, for the joy of the LORD is your strength."**
> NEH. 8:10, EMPHASIS MINE

Healing through the Anointing

When the anointing flows through us, even as we live in this secular world, the secular world will be healed. But for this to happen, we are encouraged not to compromise with the world, because we are the medicine that the world needs. The world is very sick, but we have the medicine that the world needs. This can only happen when the anointing is released through our lives.

We need to stand strong on the Word of God. The Word of God must be the standard for us and this world. The world needs to know the Word of God; otherwise, they have no hope. Because we are the true medicine, we are also the hope for this dying world.

> *Then he said to me, "This water flows toward the eastern region, goes down into the valley, and enters the sea. When it reaches the sea, its waters are healed. And it shall be that every living thing that moves, wherever the rivers go, will live. There will be a very great multitude of fish, because these waters go there; for they will be healed, and everything will live wherever the river goes."*
> EZEK. 47:8–9

Wherever the anointing flows, everything begins to live. This happens when the water enters the sea. The word *sea* here represents the world. The sea will be healed because living water will flow through the sea. This means that when the river of God flows through us, massive evangelism will take place, and there will be a great harvest. Great healings and massive deliverance will take place. The problem is that we don't have enough water flowing out of us. When the anointing flows through your life, multitudes of souls will be saved. They will all be healed. The verse specifically says that everything will live because of the anointing.

> *"It shall be that **fishermen will stand** by it from En Gedi to En Eglaim; they will be places for spreading their nets. Their fish will be of the same kinds as the fish of the Great Sea, exceedingly many."*
> EZEK. 47:10, EMPHASIS MINE

The word *fishermen* here means "all the servants of God." When the anointing flows, the servants of God will arise, and their nets will be organized and connected. This is the structure of the Kingdom of God. It does not refer to a pyramid structure, nor is it a denomination. This is where the fivefold ministry will stand, break down denominational walls, and take away all prejudice. God is calling us together in one Spirit, one faith, and one love. When this is accomplished, the power of God will begin to flow through us. There will be great fish in the great sea that we will be able to catch. God is spreading His net over all the world so that people can network with one another. We need to think about why God promised us a multitude of fish, as well as how we can bring them into the Kingdom of God. For example, if we have a network in America, and someone else has a network in Australia, and many others in different nations, then the world will be inside the net. Then we can work together and bring them into the Kingdom of God. This is why God is releasing networks right now. He does not want denominations, but networks, working together to build His Kingdom.

Chapter Eleven

Prosperity

Many people don't understand that the anointing is strongly related to prosperity. Without the power of God, there can be no prosperity. But when God releases His power through His people, they will then be blessed. Through the power of God, we can possess all the inheritance of God. Christ is the seed of Abraham, and because we are "in Christ," we have the right to receive all of the inheritance of Abraham. This is the promise of God.

The Promise of the Blessing

All the way back in Genesis 1:26–28, God created mankind and blessed them. He gave them power and authority to be fruitful and multiply, to fill the earth, and to have dominion over every living thing that moves on the earth. Because we are His children, we have the right to possess the inheritance of the Kingdom of God. Why? Because God owns everything in heaven and on earth. This truth tells us that we are wealthy! From this moment on, we should act like we have everything we need. This is what it means to have faith—and it is God's command. There is no condition involved, such as, "if we can or can't do it." We *must* do it. We have a great promise from God, and we need to act upon this promise.

> *"You say in your heart, 'My power and the might of my hand have gained me this wealth.' And you shall remember the LORD your God, for it is He who gives you power to get wealth, that He may establish His covenant which He swore to your fathers, as it is this day."*
> DEUT. 8:17–18, EMPHASIS MINE

In God, We Have Everything

What we need to understand is that we lack nothing because God has everything. God is telling us through the Spirit that we have everything. God is also telling us that He gives us the power to get wealth. But we must establish this covenant with God through a relationship. We are covenant people. We need to have an intimate relationship with God. As we foster this relationship with Him, we also need to be in relationship with others. This is the covenant relationship that we have, and it is extremely important in the body of Christ. The reason God is giving us the power to get wealth is to establish this covenant relationship.

Wealth is a resource for our safety. As we seek wealth, we need to remember that all wealth belongs to God. All resources belong to Him.

> *"Both **riches and honor come from You,**
> And You reign over all.
> In Your hand is power and might;
> In Your hand it is to make great
> And to give strength to all."*
> 1 CHRON. 29:12, EMPHASIS MINE

The God of Mammon

Money is not the problem, but the god of mammon is. Many people assume that money is the true problem. When our attention is taken away from the Lord because of money or mammon, then that's where the problem lies. *Behind* money is the god of mammon. We need to be careful that when we make money, we make it without serving the god of mammon. However, when we use the money for serving the Lord, He will give us the power to get further wealth. But if we misuse our wealth, it will cause us to sin, and our wealth will be plundered.

> *"O My mountain in the field,*
> *I will give as plunder your wealth, all your treasures,*
> *And your high places of sin within all thy borders."*
> JER. 17:3

> *"Moreover I will deliver all the wealth of this city, all its produce, and all its precious things; all the treasures of the kings of Judah I will give into the hand of their enemies, who will plunder them, seize them, and carry them to Babylon."*
> JER. 20:5

Sin brings curses into our lives. If we are living under the sin nature, we lose everything that God gave to us. We need to live holy lives. We can't compromise with the secular world. Our lives have to be changed over to God's nature. If we live by God's nature, then the inheritance will be ours. When we know who we are in God, then we can have the inheritance of God.

Where Does Wealth Come From?

> *A good man leaves an inheritance to his children's children,*
> *But the **wealth of the sinner is stored up for the righteous**.*
> PROV. 13:22, EMPHASIS MINE

This is God's promise to His people. All the wealth that the secular people make will be given to the righteous. Are you excited because of this? All of the sinners' wealth will be given to righteous people. If *we* are righteous people, the wealth will be given to us! This does not come automatically. We need the anointing in order to receive this. The anointing is the key to release the finances from the secular world to come to us.

> *For God gives wisdom and knowledge and joy to a man*
> *who is good in His sight; but to the sinner He gives the*
> *work of gathering and collecting, that he may give to*
> *him who is good before God.*
> ECCL. 2:26

God causes the sinners to work and gather all of what they make, and ultimately give it to those who are pleasing in His sight. Do you believe this truth? Do you really believe that the wealth of the sinners is for us? It is as if they are holding our wealth for us.

> *Here is what I have seen: It is good and fitting for one to*
> *eat and drink, and to enjoy the good of all his labor in*
> *which he toils under the sun all the days of his life which*
> *God gives him; for it is his heritage. As for every man to*
> *whom **God has** **given riches and wealth, and given him***
> ***power to eat** of it, to receive his heritage and rejoice in*
> *his labor—**this is the gift of God.** For he will not dwell*
> *unduly on the days of his life, because God keeps him*
> *busy with the joy of his heart.*
> ECCL. 5:18–20, EMPHASIS MINE

When God is pleased with your life, He will give you wisdom, knowledge, and joy. We know that Jesus Christ, the Son of God, is a gift to us, and the Holy Spirit is also a gift of God. The Old Testament states that riches and wealth are gifts from God. We need to believe and proclaim this promise. We need to see that there is a bright future ahead of us. If we're busy and we have joy in life, we don't have to worry about tomorrow.

Prosperity

Every man should eat and drink and enjoy the good of all his labor—it is the gift of God.

We need to enjoy our life in God! Every Christian needs to have this power.

How to Handle Wealth

We should not think that being wealthy is everything there is to life.

> *Then God said to him: "Because you have asked this thing, and have not asked long life for yourself, nor have asked riches for yourself, nor have asked the life of your enemies, but have asked for yourself understanding to discern justice, behold, I have done according to your words; see, I have given you a wise and understanding heart, so that there has not been anyone like you before you, nor shall any like you arise after you. And I have also given you what you have not asked: both riches and honor, so that there shall not be anyone like you among the kings all your days."*
> 1 KINGS 3:11–13

We should not trust in our wealth alone.

> *Here is the man who did not make God his strength,*
> *But trusted in the abundance of his riches,*
> *And strengthened himself in his wickedness*
> PS. 52:7

We need to put our trust in God. All the resources of wealth come from God. Do not pour out your heart after wealth.

> *Vindicate me, O LORD,*
> *For I have walked in my integrity.*
> *I have also trusted in the LORD;*
> *I shall not slip.*
> PS. 26:1

Do not trust in oppression,
Nor vainly hope in robbery;
If riches increase,
Do not set your heart on them.

Ps. 62:10

Also, do not seek abundant wealth. Be satisfied with what you have.

Remove falsehood and lies far from me;
Give me neither poverty nor riches—
Feed me with the food allotted to me;
Lest I be full and deny You,
And say, "Who is the LORD?"
Or lest I be poor and steal,
And profane the name of my God.

PROV. 30:8–9

Many people are seeking abundant blessings. Remember, we have everything because of who is inside of us. We lack nothing in our lives. If you're seeking God, He will supply all the needs of your life.

And my God shall supply all your need according to His
riches in glory by Christ Jesus.

PHIL. 4:19

We need to use our wealth by offering it to God.

In a great trial of affliction the abundance of their joy
and their deep poverty abounded in the riches of their
liberality.

2 COR. 8:2

We need to remember why God has brought material blessings into our lives. We need to believe that God will supply all of our needs. We should, however, not despise wealth.

A feast is made for laughter,
And wine makes merry;
But money answers everything.
Do not curse the king, even in your thought;
Do not curse the rich, even in your bedroom;
For a bird of the air may carry your voice,
And a bird in flight may tell the matter.
ECCL. 10:19–20

If someone is poor, that person shouldn't despise another person who is wealthy. This is not the type of attitude that will get you wealth. We need to thank God that the other person is wealthy. God promised to Abraham that whatever he saw and whatever he heard was for him. God has a purpose for bringing wealthy people into your life. It's not a coincidence. God always brings His divine appointments into our lives. We may not know our steps, but God knows exactly where we are to go.

Wealth can also lead to corruption. We need to warn people of the corruption that it produces.

Come now, you rich, weep and howl for your miseries
that are coming upon you! Your riches are corrupted,
and your garments are moth-eaten. Your gold and silver
are corroded, and their corrosion will be a witness against
you and will eat your flesh like fire. You have heaped up
treasure in the last days. Indeed the wages of the labor-
ers who mowed your fields, which you kept back by fraud,
cry out; and the cries of the reapers have reached the
ears of the Lord of Sabaoth. You have lived on the earth
in pleasure and luxury; you have fattened your hearts as
in a day of slaughter. You have condemned, you have
murdered the just; he does not resist you.
JAMES 5:1–6

Don't focus on wealth, but instead put your trust in the Lord.

For the love of money is a root of all kinds of evil, for which some have strayed from the faith in their greediness, and pierced themselves through with many sorrows.... Command those who are rich in this present age not to be haughty, nor to trust in uncertain riches but in the living God, who gives us richly all things to enjoy.

1 TIM. 6:10, 17

The Purpose of Wealth

Wealth is meant to be used to extend God's Kingdom. When the Israelites came out from the land of Egypt, God gave them special favor by causing all of the Egyptians to release their silver, gold, and other special jewelry to the Israelites.

Then the LORD spoke to Moses, saying: "Speak to the children of Israel, that they bring Me an offering. From everyone who gives it willingly with his heart you shall take My offering. And this is the offering which you shall take from them: gold, silver, and bronze; blue, purple, and scarlet thread, fine linen, and goats' hair; ram skins dyed red, badger skins, and acacia wood; oil for the light, and spices for anointing oil and for the sweet incense; onyx stones, and stones to be set in the ephod and in the breastplate.

Ex. 25:1–7

God gave those things to the Israelites for only one purpose: to build the tabernacle of God. All the wealth that the Israelites obtained had originally belonged to the Egyptians. God designed it that way so that they could build His temple. The reason God blesses us with wealth is to build His temple and extend His Kingdom. It is also used to help the poor, the widows, and the orphans.

He has dispersed abroad,
He has given to the poor;
His righteousness endures forever;

His horn will be exalted with honor.
Ps. 112:9

Another reason is to do good business for God.

Let them do good, that they be rich in good works, ready
to give, willing to share.
1 Tim. 6:18

When the glory of God manifests, then all material blessings will be transferred to the body of Christ.

Then you shall see and become radiant,
And your heart shall swell with joy;
Because the abundance of the sea shall be turned to you,
The wealth of the Gentiles shall come to you.
Isa. 60:5

All different types of blessings will be transferred to us. We need to understand the plan God has for the body of Christ. This plan will not take place automatically. We need to arise and shine in the darkness with the glory of God. As we shine with God's glory, then all of the blessings of this world, including the wealth of the Gentiles, will come to us. Christians should not worry, because even though this world is getting darker, God has promised that He will cover this world with His glory. Hallelujah! Then the scripture passage above will be fulfilled in our lives.

Wealth Is Connected with Power Evangelism

The anointing of God demonstrated through power evangelism will bring prosperity. Wealth and power evangelism always go together; they can't be separated. If you want a big crusade, you will not be able to accomplish that without money. Power evangelism always requires the anointing of God, which, in turn, releases material blessings.

"Thus says the Lord to His anointed,
To Cyrus, whose right hand I have held—
To subdue nations before him
And loose the armor of kings,
To open before him the double doors,
So that the gates will not be shut:
'I will go before you
And make the crooked places straight;
I will break in pieces the gates of bronze
And cut the bars of iron.
I will give you the treasures of darkness
And hidden riches of secret places,
That you may know that I, the Lord,
Who call you by your name,
Am the God of Israel."

Isa. 45:1–3

In this passage, King Cyrus was the anointed one of God. With that anointing, God was able to release the treasures of darkness and the hidden riches of secret places to him.

Today, we are the anointed ones of God. Because we are the anointed ones, all of the material blessings, which are the treasures of darkness and the hidden riches in secret places, now belong to us. We must proclaim that all the treasures of darkness and hidden riches will come to us in the name of Jesus Christ. We can proclaim this because it is God's promise to us, and any promises of God that He has made, we can proclaim. We should make it a daily prayer to command these treasures of darkness and hidden riches to come to the Kingdom of God, and also to our lives.

Judah also will fight at Jerusalem.
*And **the wealth of all the surrounding nations***
Shall be gathered together:
*Gold, silver, and apparel **in great abundance**.*

Zech. 14:14, emphasis mine

From all surrounding nations, God will gather their wealth in great abundance. Does this excite you? The previous verses give us even further insight:

> *It shall be one day*
> *Which is known to the LORD—*
> *Neither day nor night.*
> *But at evening time it shall happen*
> *That it will be light.*
> *And in that day it shall be*
> *That living waters shall flow from Jerusalem,*
> *Half of them toward the eastern sea*
> *And half of them toward the western sea;*
> *In both summer and winter it shall occur.*
> *And the LORD shall be King over all the earth.*
> *In that day it shall be—*
> *"The LORD is one,"*
> *And His name one.*
> ZECH. 14:7–9

When God is the King of all the nations, then the surrounding nations' wealth shall be gathered together and be given to us—abundantly! We need to release the anointing inside of our hearts. What is the key to releasing this anointing? Joy! Remember the water that flows from the Garden of Eden. *Eden* means "pleasure and joy." That's why the joy of the Lord is our strength. The apostle Paul tells us to rejoice always. Rejoice, rejoice, and rejoice! That is the key to releasing the anointing.

CONCLUSION

I have discussed many things in this book. As Christians, if we don't know who we are in Christ, we will miss out on what God has in store for us. You are here for a reason! God has given everyone a destiny to fulfill. You were not put here on earth by accident. God has designed something great for your life. It is imperative that we know who we are in Christ.

We need to be excited about the future. The future holds great things for God's people. We should not worry or be fearful of the future, but we should have a great expectation that a move of God is about to take place. God is raising up people who will have a confident assurance of who they are in Christ. These are the people whom God is ready to use. God is looking for people who have a firm foundation in Christ.

The Bible clearly states that the harvest is plentiful, but the workers are few. So we need to pray for more laborers. Are you one of those laborers whom God wants to use? Are you excited about a great harvest in the future? Do you know now that you possess something that is far greater than what the world has to offer? It is because of Him with whom you are affiliated that you have a true calling in life.

Knowing your identity can bring you to your ultimate destination. It is the driving force in your life that will give you the assurance of what life is really all about. Are you ready to go out there and judge this world? Can you be a vessel ready to be used to bring about the greatest move of God in this age? We need to arise, shine, and show forth the glory of God. This will only take place through your behavior and attitude in this world. God has called each and every one of us to be judges. Are you ready to judge the world? The power is already in you. You simply need to believe and go out in faith and proclaim the praise of God.

Another word of encouragement is that we need the anointing more than ever. The anointing is the key to everything. It holds the success of our future. Without the anointing of God, we would not be able to do anything. Just as the apostle Paul tells us to desire spiritual gifts, we need to earnestly desire the anointing in our life. Each new day will bring a fresh, new anointing. We must rely on the anointing of God. We must not be people who constantly lose this power. The most powerful Being in the universe is residing inside of us, and there is nothing that will be able to stop us. Your destiny *will* be fulfilled.

Now, are you filled with joy? God desires His people to live with joy. The joy of the Lord must be our strength if we want to see great things happen in our life. Once you know your identity, you can fulfill your calling as a judge of this world. Hallelujah!

ABOUT THE AUTHOR

Israel Kim

Israel Kim came to America in the early eighties to obtain a doctorate degree in International Business. However, God called him instead to be a minister of the Gospel of Jesus Christ. Since 1984, he has been involved in ministry with the Southern Baptist denomination, and later moved to an affiliation with the Assembly of God ministries. He is ordained under the International Ministerial Association and Apostolic Resource Ministries.

His ministry is based upon the leading of the Holy Spirit to represent the heavenly Father. He has been providing apostolic and prophetic oversight, and he has covered many churches and ministers in many different nations. As he has traveled across the world, thousands and thousands of souls have been saved, healed, and delivered in his ministry. Miracles, signs, and wonders have been manifested as a "usual" part of his ministry—dead people even have been raised. During a meeting in Moscow, 1,200 people were miraculously healed in one night.

Throughout twenty years of ministry experience, he has provided a well-balanced, biblical approach to the restoration of the office of the apostle, in which he has functioned for the last fifteen years. He is the co-founder, with his wife, and currently serves as the president of Apostles Ministries and as the executive director of Apostles Ministries Empowerment Network.

He formerly served as a dean of St. Petersburg Christian College, and he currently serves as the chancellor of the International School of Apostles. He has also taught at several seminaries and Bible colleges in several countries. He is a member of the International Coalition of Apostles (presiding apostle: C. Peter Wagner), and a member of the Apostolic Council for Educational Accountability.

He and his wife, Rebekah, and daughter, Gloria, reside in Sterling, Virginia.

TO CONTACT THE AUTHOR
Apostles Ministries Empowerment Network
P.O. Box 10166
McLean, VA 22102 (USA)
Phone: 703-893-5399
Fax: 703-893-3958
E-mail: apostle7@4amen.org

International School of Apostles
1-5-3F, Minamisaiwai-cho, Saiwai-ku,
Kawasaki-shi, Kanagawa, Japan 212-0061
Tel/Fax: 81-44-533-1240 (Japan)
E-mail: isoa@cronos.ocn.ne.jp
www.4amen.org